The Legend of Sir Gawain; Studies Upon its Original Scope and Significance

Grimm Library

No. 7

THE LEGEND OF SIR GAWAIN

GRIMM LIBRARY. No. 1.

GEORGIAN FOLK-TALES. Translated by MARJORY WARDROP.
Cr. 8vo, pp. xii + 175. 5s. *net.*

GRIMM LIBRARY No. 2.

THE LEGEND OF PERSEUS. By EDWIN SIDNEY HARTLAND, F.S.A.
VOL. I. THE SUPERNATURAL BIRTH.
Cr. 8vo, pp. xxxiv + 228. 7s. 6d. *net.*

GRIMM LIBRARY. No. 3.

THE LEGEND OF PERSEUS. By EDWIN SIDNEY HARTLAND, F.S.A.
VOL. II. THE LIFE-TOKEN.
Cr. 8vo, pp. viii + 445. 12s. 6d. *net.*

GRIMM LIBRARY. No. 4.

THE VOYAGE OF BRAN, SON OF FEBAL. Edited by KUNO MEYER. With an Essay upon the Happy Otherworld in Irish Myth, by ALFRED NUTT. Vol. I.
Cr. 8vo, pp. xvii + 331. 10s. 6d. *net.*

GRIMM LIBRARY. No. 5.

THE LEGEND OF PERSEUS. By EDWIN SIDNEY HARTLAND, F.S.A.
VOL. III. ANDROMEDA. MEDUSA
Cr. 8vo, pp. xxxvii + 225. 7s. 6d. *net.*

GRIMM LIBRARY. No. 6.

THE VOYAGE OF BRAN, SON OF FEBAL. Edited by KUNO MEYER. With Essays upon the Irish Vision of the Happy Otherworld, and the Celtic Doctrine of Rebirth, by ALFRED NUTT. Vol. II.
Cr. 8vo, pp. xii + 352. 10s. 6d. *net.*

All rights reserved

THE
Legend of Sir Gawain

STUDIES UPON ITS ORIGINAL
SCOPE AND SIGNIFICANCE: BY

Jessie L. Weston

TRANSLATOR OF WOLFRAM VON
ESCHENBACH'S 'PARZIVAL'

'Sir Gawayne hath sought the isles of light
 Beyond the shores of day,
Where morn never waneth to shades of night,
 And the silver fountains play;
There he holdeth high court as the Maidens' Knight,
 In the Maidens' Isle for aye'

Published by David Nutt
in the Strand, London
1897

PN
686
G3
W53
A.1c9793
S

E B

Edinburgh. T and A Constable, Printers to Her Majesty

AUTHOR'S PREFACE

IN presenting these Studies to the public a few words of explanation may be necessary. They were undertaken solely with the object stated in the Introductory Chapter—that of throwing light upon the Arthurian cycle as a whole, by ascertaining, if possible, what was the precise nature of the tradition originally associated with the knight who played so important a part in that cycle. I had formed no definite conclusion on the subject—the results, such as they are, have evolved themselves naturally and inevitably in the course of careful study and comparison of the different stories.

If these results seem to point to a Celtic origin as represented in *Gaelic* (Irish) rather than *Kymric* (Welsh) literature, to a mode of transmission in which specifically *Welsh* tradition has played apparently but little part, I would ask the reader to believe that such results are in no sense due to a previous bias towards, or against, the conclusions of any individual scholar, or group of scholars.

I do not claim to do more than bring together facts which, hitherto scattered, may, in their collected form, help to elucidate a highly confused and perplexing section of the Arthurian cycle, and at the same time suggest an interpretation of these facts which appears to me to be neither forced nor unnatural. But it may be that though the evidence, as I interpret it, appears to me to point clearly in one direction, others better versed in such matters may read it otherwise. In the present state of Arthurian investigation that writer is over-bold who claims infallibility, or finality, for the most tempting conclusions.

It only remains for me to express my indebtedness to those scholars whose works have been of use to me in preparing these Studies, and especially to Mr. Alfred Nutt, to whose advice and valuable suggestions this book, in its completed form, owes much.

JESSIE L. WESTON.

BOURNEMOUTH, *August* 1897.

CONTENTS

CHAPTER I

INTRODUCTORY

The Arthurian legend in England—Arthur, historical and mythical—Necessity of examining the legends connected with the leading knights 1

CHAPTER II

EARLY CONCEPTIONS OF GAWAIN

William of Malmesbury—Testimony of Italian records—Gradual declension of Gawain's character—Inconsistency of Malory's presentation—Gawain originally Celtic—Peculiarity ascribed to him—Probably a solar hero—Gringalet—Excalibur . . 7

CHAPTER III

THE LEGEND IN CHRÉTIEN'S 'CONTE DEL GRAAL' AND WOLFRAM'S 'PARZIVAL'

Summary of the two poems—Wolfram's conclusion probably independent and genuine 18

CHAPTER IV

THE LEGEND IN THE MINOR ROMANCES

General character of the incidents most frequently alluded to—List of such incidents—The romances in which they occur—Parallel with Cuchulinn's adventures in *The Wooing of Emer* . . 26

CHAPTER V

THE MAGIC CASTLE

The Castle in Chrétien and Wolfram—Castles regarded as otherworld dwellings—The lady and the magician—The Isle of Women—*Diu Krône*—*The Voyage of Bran*—Death of Gawain, real and supposed—Gawain in Fairyland—Apparition of Gawain to Arthur—Real significance of the Château Merveil adventure—Visit to the other-world in Teutonic and Celtic mythology—Position of this adventure in the Gawain legend   32

CHAPTER VI

THE LOVES OF GAWAIN

No special lady connected with Gawain—Conflicting testimony on the point—Gawain's character affected by the 'Castle' adventure—His love a supernatural maiden—Her connection with a magician—*Diu Krône*—Cuchulinn—This feature preserved in English romances—*The Marriage of Syr Gawayne*—Interesting Irish parallel—The Loathly Messenger—*The Carle of Carlile*—Summary of evidence—Its bearing on the question of transmission of the Arthurian legend   44

CHAPTER VII

GAWAIN'S SON

Testimony of romances on this point—The *Fair Unknown* cycle—General summary of story—Hero's youth—*Libeaus Desconus*—*Le Bel Inconnu*—*Carduino*—*Wigalois*—His connection with Perceval—Views of Dr. Schofield and M. Ferd Lot—His parentage—Superior antiquity of the *Danae* motif—Connection between Gawain and Perceval—Tradition of conflict between father and son—Its bearing on the Gawain legend   .   .   .   55

CONTENTS

CHAPTER VIII

LE CHEVALIER DE LA CHARRETTE

Different versions of the story—Chrêtien—Hartmann von Aue—Malory—Suggestions as to original hero—Professor Rhys—M. Gaston Paris—Gawain's share in the adventure—The character of Meléagaunt's kingdom—*Li pons evages*—Pierre Bercheur—Early connection of Gawain and Guinevere—Survival in English metrical romances—Gawain and Lancelot—Perceval and Galahad 67

CHAPTER IX

SIR GAWAIN AND THE GREEN KNIGHT

Summary of the English poem—*Li Conte del Graal*—*Diu Krône*—*La Mule sans Frein*—The prose *Perceval*—The *Fled Bricrend*—Antiquity of the story—Comparison of the various forms—Examination of the *Carados* version—Identification of the Knight-Magician—Original significance of the story—Probable order of the different versions—The magic girdle—The story probably a genuine survival of original Gawain legend . . 85

CHAPTER X

THE LEGEND IN MALORY

Importance of Malory's version as drawn from all the principal branches of Arthurian literature—Testimony of each section to early Perceval-Gawain story—Passages in illustration—Their bearing on the relations between Chrêtien and Wolfram—Concluding summary of results deduced from these studies . . 103

INDEX 113

ERRATUM

Page 8, line 6, *for* Walwain *read* Walwein.

LIST OF BOOKS CONSULTED

TEXTS

Li Conte del Graal. Poem by Chrêtien de Troyes. With the continuations of Gautier de Doulens, Gerbert, and Manessier. Printed by Potvin from a MS. in the Mons Library. Mons, 1866-71. Six volumes. Vol. contains the prose romance of *Perceval li Gallois*, by an unknown writer.

Parzival. Poem by Wolfram von Eschenbach. Edited by Karl Bartsch. (*Deutsche Classiker des Mittelalters*, vols. ix. x. xi.) Leipzig, 1875-79.

    ∴ The translated passages are from the author's English rendering. 2 vols. London, 1894.

Le Roman de Merlin. Edited from the French MS., Add. 10292, in the British Museum, by Dr. H. Oskar Sommer. London, 1894.

Le Morte d'Arthur, by Syr Thomas Malory. The original edition of William Caxton reprinted and edited by Dr. H. Oskar Sommer. London, 1889-92. Three volumes. Vol. i. Text. Vol. iii. Studies on the Sources. (Vol. ii. has not been referred to.)

Diu Krône. Poem by Heinrich von dem Turlin. Edited by J. H. F. Scholl. Stuttgart, 1852.

Iwein oder *Der Ritter mit dem Löwen.* Poem by Hartmann von Aue. Edited by Fedor Bech. *Deutsche Classiker des Mittelalters,* vol. vi. Leipzig, 1888.

Syr Gawayne. A collection of ancient Romance-poems by Scottish and English authors, relating to that celebrated Knight of the Round Table. Edited by Sir Frederick Madden. Printed for the Bannatyne Club. London, 1839.

Histoire Littéraire de la France, vol. xxx. Romans en vers du Cycle de la Table Ronde. (Introductory essay and study of the different romances by M. Gaston Paris.) Paris, 1888.

.·. Contains summaries of the following romances quoted in this work: *La Mule sans Frein*; *Le cimetière perilleux*; *Rigomer*; *La vengeance de Raguidel*; and of many others referring to Gawain.

MONOGRAPHS

HARTLAND (E. S.). The Legend of Perseus. Vol. i. The Supernatural Birth. London, 1894.

NUTT (ALFRED). The Aryan Expulsion and Return Formula in the Folk- and Hero-tales of the Celts (*Folk-lore Record,* vol. iv. London, 1882.)

—— Studies on the Legend of the Holy Grail, with especial reference to the hypothesis of its Celtic origin. London, 1888.

—— and K. Meyer. The Voyage of Bran. Vol. i. The Happy Otherworld. London, 1895.

LIST OF BOOKS CONSULTED xiii

PARIS (GASTON). Études sur les romans de la Table Ronde (*Romania*, vols. x. and xii.). Paris, 1881, 1883.

∴ These Studies are concerned wholly with Lancelot.

RHYS (JOHN). Studies in the Arthurian Legend. London, 1891.

SCHOFIELD (W. H.). Studies on *Libeaus Desconus* (Harvard Studies and Notes in Philology and Literature, vol. iv.). Boston, 1895.

Cf. the reviews by Monsieur Ferd. Lot (*Moyen Age*, Oct. 1896), and Monsieur E. Philipot (*Romania*, April 1897).

ZIMMER (HEINRICH). Keltische Studien, V.: Ueber dem compilatorischen Character der irischen Sagentexte im sogennanten Lebor na h-Uidhre. (*Zeitschrift für vgl. Sprachforschung*, vol. xxviii. Heft 5-6.) Gutersloh, 1887.

∴ Contains summaries of the tales concerning Cuchulinn referred to in this work.

—— Göttingische gelehrte Anzeigen, 1890, No. 12. (Contains a review of Mr. Nutt's Studies on the Legend of the Holy Grail.)

—— Göttingische gelehrte Anzeigen, 1890, No. 20. (Contains a review of vol. xxx. of the *Histoire Littéraire de la France*.)

—— Bretonische Elemente in der Arthursage des Gottfried von Monmouth, and Beiträge zur Namenforschung in den altfranz Arthurepen. (*Zeitschrift für französische Sprache und Litteratur*, vol. xiii. Heft 1.)

∴ The Arthurian studies of Professor Zimmer have been vigorously criticised and, to a great extent, entirely refuted by (1) Monsieur J. Loth: Les nouvelles théories sur l'origine des romans Arthuriens (*Revue Celtique*, vol. xiii.); and (2) Monsieur Ferd. Lot: Celtica (*Romania*, vol. xxiv.); Études sur la provenance du cycle Arthurien (*Romania*, vols. xxiv. and xxv.). Cf. also Mr. Alfred Nutt's Les derniers travaux allemands sur la légende du Saint Graal (*Revue Celtique*, vol. xii.). But in the present condition of Celtic studies the summaries of texts given in Professor Zimmer's articles, the wealth of illustrative material, and the attempted identification of names, are extremely useful.

THE LEGEND OF SIR GAWAIN

Arthurian poems and Idylls has freed us from a well-deserved reproach, though, from a critical point of view, it must be admitted that his work is open to much the same objection as is Malory's—it is admirable considered as *literature*, as *legend* it does even less justice to the original characters of the story.

This feature of the question, viz., that the great mass of Arthurian romance is in a foreign tongue, ought to be borne in mind; it goes far to explain the fact—for it is a fact—that the labours of English scholars in this field have hitherto been productive of less solid results than have been achieved either in France or in Germany. It must be admitted that it strikes an English student disagreeably to find that, in taking up the study of a subject so essentially national in spirit, the English books which can be relied upon for information are so few in number, and, with some honourable exceptions, of so little value in comparison with the foreign literature.

It has long been a matter of discussion whether there ever were an historical Arthur or not. Our minds are not so easily satisfied as was Caxton's—who tells us, in his preface to Malory's *Morte d'Arthur*, how he hesitated whether to print the romance or not, doubting whether Arthur had ever lived; but was reassured by those who had seen the King's tomb at Glastonbury, and Gawain's skull at Dover Castle. Such evidence as this would scarcely satisfy us nowadays, though for the sake of English literature we may well rejoice that it satisfied Caxton.

But without committing ourselves to a faith in these interesting relics, or in Arthur's victories far afield, we may, so scholars tell us, believe that he really lived, and was a valiant warrior and successful general. Both Professor

4 THE LEGEND OF SIR GAWAIN

Rhys[1] and Mr. Alfred Nutt[2] adhere to the view that the historic Arthur occupied a position equivalent to that of the *Comes Britanniæ*, who under the Romans held a roving commission to defend the province wherever attacked. It is quite in keeping with this identification that we find Arthur warring in all parts of the island: now in Northumberland—crossing the border into Scotland to take counsel with the allied princes for an attack on the Saxons; now journeying southward to give the invaders battle on Salisbury Plain.

That mythical elements also entered largely into the popular conception of Arthur is doubtless true, as the curious story of his birth and election to the crown seem to testify,[3] but whether he really represents a Celtic God or Culture Hero,[4] or is a representative of a widespread Aryan myth,[5] we have but scanty data to determine.

Dr. Oskar Sommer predicts[6] that when all the leading MSS. of the cycle have been carefully edited, and all the romances dissected and compared, we shall find that the original Arthur saga is very simple in form,—it is the stories connected with the other heroes who gathered round the British king, which have crossed and complicated the primitive legend. One, and that an important step in the great work of elucidating this confused tangle of romance, would therefore be the careful sifting of the stories connected with the individual knights; the attempt to discover what was the *original* form of each legend; to find out, if

---

[1] *Studies in the Arthurian Legend*, chap. i.
[2] *Mabinogion Studies*; Folklore Record, vol. v.
[3] Cf. *Merlin*, chaps. v. and vi.   [4] Rhys, *Studies*.
[5] Nutt, *Aryan Expulsion and Return Formula*; Folklore Record, vol. iv.   [6] Introduction to the *Merlin*, p. viii.

we can, how much they have borrowed—in the case of the leading knights, how much they have lent; and thus by separating, as far as may be, the threads of the fabric, to discover the nature of the ground-work. But this is a task which is only practicable, and indeed only serviceable, in the case of the leading figures of the legend—such characters as Gawain, Perceval, Kay, Tristan, Lancelot, and Galahad. The great crowd of minor characters who cross and recross the stage are in many instances only understudies of the principal heroes; their adventures but reflections of deeds originally attributed to other and more important actors in the drama. Many of these characters would well repay study of the details of their story, but in the case of those above named the work is not merely desirable, but absolutely essential, if we are ever to arrive at a clear idea of the growth of this great legend.

Something has already been done in this direction. Mr. Nutt's *Studies on the Legend of the Holy Grail* have gone far towards the elucidation of the original *données* of the Perceval story. Professor Zimmer's study on the Tristan saga has thrown light upon the genesis of that legend; but there is still a vast field to be explored. The most perplexing, and in many ways the most important, of all the knights surrounding King Arthur, Gawain, has hitherto failed to meet with the favour accorded to his companions; true, the materials for an examination of his legend have in a great measure been prepared by Sir Frederick Madden[1] in his collection of English metrical romances, and by M. Gaston Paris,[2] in his study of the episodic romances connected with the hero; but the varying legends have

[1] *Sir Gawayne*, Madden, printed for Bannatyne Club.
[2] *Histoire Littéraire de la France*, vol. xxx.

not hitherto been examined and compared with a view to determining what was the original form of the Gawain Legend.

The more one studies the Arthurian cycle, the more one becomes convinced of the importance of this character, and of the necessity of discovering his original *rôle*. The materials at our disposal grow with every year, and we are now far better furnished for the task than was the case when Sir Frederick Madden undertook to collect the romances connected with Sir Gawain. These Studies therefore have been undertaken with the view of leading to a truer appreciation of one of the most puzzling, and at the same time most fascinating, characters of the Arthurian cycle, a character which later developments of the legend have greatly obscured, and most unjustly vilified. If in the course of these Studies certain points are established which may impel those better qualified than the present writer to pursue the investigation yet further, they will have amply fulfilled their object.

CHAPTER II

EARLY CONCEPTIONS OF GAWAIN

William of Malmesbury—Testimony of Italian records—Gradual declension of Gawain's character—Inconsistency of Malory's presentation—Gawain originally Celtic—Peculiarity ascribed to him—Probably a solar hero—Gringalet—Excalibur.

THERE is practically no doubt that, as mentioned in the previous chapter, the Arthurian legend proper has become greatly obscured by the introduction of legends connected with other heroes; there is but little more doubt that the first of all the heroes with whom Arthur gradually became connected was he whom we know from the Anglo-Norman and French romances as *Walwein, Gauvain, Gawain,* and from Welsh texts as *Gwalchmai.* The first M. Gaston Paris looks upon as the oldest form of the name by which the knight is best known, and it is no unusual thing to find *both* Walwein and Gawain employed in the same romance. That the French *Gawain* and Welsh *Gwalchmai* are the same character is certain, but the connection of these two forms is not so clear.

Any student of the Arthurian cycle could, without difficulty, name romances in which such leading heroes as Tristan, Lancelot, or Galahad are not even mentioned, but it would be difficult to recall one in which *Gawain* does not figure,—sometimes even more prominently than the ostensible hero of the romance. Always closely connected with Arthur, his uncle on the mother's side, he is found in the historical accounts of that king, even as in the romantic. M. Gaston Paris gives,[1] as the earliest mention of him, a quotation from William of Malmesbury (1125), relating to the discovery of Walwain's tomb at Ross in Pembrokeshire; he is there mentioned as Arthur's nephew, and 'not unworthy of Arthur.' Professor Zimmer, in his criticism of M. Paris' views,[2] carries the literary evidence further back, by referring to Signor Rajna's discovery of names of Breton heroes in Italian deeds of the early twelfth century; *Artusius* (*Arthur*) and *Galvanus* (*Gawain*) are names of frequent recurrence. The German scholar is of opinion that these names justify the conclusion that the heroes were well known in Italy by 1090—arguing a widespread continental acquaintance with the romances during the last thirty years of the eleventh century, at the latest —a date considerably anterior to that of any romance we now possess.[3] Of those which have descended to us we may take Chrêtien de Troyes' poems both as the earliest in themselves, and as representing a more primitive and less complicated form of the respective stories with which they deal. In all these poems, and also in the earlier prose romances, such as the *Merlin* (even in its extended form), Gawain appears as the *beau-idéal* of courage and courtesy, and this character he preserves in the English metrical

---

[1] *Hist. Litt. de la France*, vol. xxx. p. 29; Madden, *Sir Gawayne*, Introd. p. xxiv.

[2] *Gottingische Gelehrte Anzeigen*, 1890, No. 20, p. 831.

[3] The Italians derived their knowledge of Arthur and his knights from the Normans, who conquered Sicily and South Italy in the first half of the eleventh century, and these in their turn must have heard the stories from their Breton neighbours.

romances. But in the later stage of the Arthur-saga, in those versions which are devoted to the most highly developed and ecclesiasticised form of the Grail legend, the character of Gawain undergoes a remarkable and striking change: he becomes a mere libertine, cruel and treacherous.

Even his valour is no longer unquestioned. In the earlier romances Gawain is practically invincible; at the most, as in the case of Iwein,[1] his opponent succeeds in achieving a drawn battle. Wirnt von Gravenberg, in his *Wigalois*, apologises eagerly for having repeated in his poems a statement to the effect that Gawain had been defeated by an unknown knight; if he had not been assured of it by his authority he would never have ventured to do so.[2]

In the *Suite de Merlin* we find the enchanter prophesying Gawain's glory, and foretelling that he shall only be overcome by *one* knight; but when we reach Malory (Book iv. chap. 18) we find a list of *six* knights, each of whom has proved superior in valour to the once invincible hero.

But Malory, who drew from various sources, and represents a late stage in the evolution of the legend, is remarkably inconsistent in his treatment of Gawain; the earlier and later conceptions strive together in his version, and he makes statements utterly at variance the one with the other. Thus in Books vii. chap. 35, and x.[3] chap. 58, we find Gareth refusing to have anything to do with his

---

[1] Chrétien de Troyes, *Le Chevalier au Lion*; Hartmann von Aue, *Der Löwen Ritter*.

[2] Schofield, *Studies on the Libeaus Desconus*, p. 221. See also on this point M. G. Paris' remarks, *Hist. Litt.*, xxx. p. 32.

[3] Book x., drawn from the *Tristan*.

10 THE LEGEND OF SIR GAWAIN

brother Gawain, on the ground that he is *treacherous, vengeable, a murderer of good knights*, and *a hater of all knights of the Round Table*; while, in Book xiii.[1] chap. 16, Gawain and Gareth ride together in search of the Grail; and in Book xx.[2] chap. 1, Gawain, Gareth, and Gaheris together refuse to countenance Mordred and Agravain in their betrayal of Lancelot and Guinevere to King Arthur. It is in revenge for the death of Gareth at Lancelot's hands that Gawain urges the King to the fatal war with Lancelot; he can forgive the death of his sons, but not that of his dearly loved brother. And, when Gawain himself dies, both Arthur and Lancelot lament him in terms utterly out of keeping with Malory's previous indications; to Arthur he is *the man in the world I loved most*; to Lancelot, *a ful noble knyght as ever was borne*.[3] It is not easy to account for this change in the estimation in which Gawain was held; Sir F. Madden thinks that the original offender was the compiler of the prose *Tristan*, who desired to exalt the fame of his special hero at the expense of the better-known Gawain. It seems, however, more probable that the reason may rather be sought in the strongly moralising tendencies of the later romances, there being certain features of the original Gawain story difficult

---

[1] Drawn from the *Queste*.

[2] Drawn from the prose *Lancelot* and *Morte d'Arthur*.

[3] In the face of these facts it is extraordinary that writers persist in asserting that Malory's presentation of Gawain is an entirely unfavourable one. It is still more extraordinary that any critic familiar with the text should assert that Malory has himself conceived an entirely original presentation of the character, yet this is what Sir Ed. Strachey affirms. Malory's Gawain is a tissue of inconsistencies, entirely due to the variety of sources consulted, and the lack of any attempt to harmonise these sources.

EARLY CONCEPTIONS OF GAWAIN

to combine with edification. If it were the author of the *Tristan* only who was in fault, we should expect to find the old conception of Gawain obtaining in romances not affected by the *Tristan*, but all the later versions show this same declension.

But, whatever the original reason, it is unfortunately the case that later writers have followed in the track of Malory rather than in that of Chrêtien; and the English nineteenth-century representations of Gawain are even more unjust to the original than are the fifteenth. Tennyson depicts him as *light of love, false, reckless*, and *irreverent*; and when we find Morris[1] speaking of *gloomy Gawain*, we have indeed travelled far from the early English *Sir Gawayne*, the *gay, gratious*, and *gude*,[2] who

> '*plus volt faire que il ne dist,*
> *Et plus doner qu'il ne promist.*'[3]

Scholars are now practically unanimous in admitting that, though the development of Gawain as a model of chivalrous knighthood is due largely to the Northern French poets, the character is, in its origin, Celtic. M. Gaston Paris says that Gawain belongs '*certainement à la tradition celtique la plus ancienne*';[4] but what was the special '*tradition celtique*' relating to the hero it is now difficult to say. The very popularity which Gawain so long enjoyed has operated disastrously, by making him the hero of such a perplexing crowd of adventures that it might well seem labour thrown away to endeavour to separate from the mass any incidents which may be regarded as forming the

---

[1] *Defence of Guinevere.*
[2] *Gologras and Gawain*, v. x.; Madden, p. 136.
[3] Wace, *Brut*, vol. ii. p. 80; *Hist. Litt.*, p. 32.
[4] *Hist. Litt.*, xxx. p. 29.

kernel, so to speak, of his story, and yet, at the outset, he must have been the hero of certain definite adventures, certain special feats, which caused him to be looked upon as worthy to be allied with the hero-king of the Britons. It is possible that at first he may have been even a more notable hero than Arthur himself.

It ought not to be impossible to single out from among the various versions of Gawain's adventures certain features which, by their frequent recurrence in the romances devoted to him, and their analogy to ancient Celtic tradition, seem as if they might with probability be regarded as forming part of his original story. It is scarcely to be hoped that we can ever construct a coherent account on which we may lay our finger and say '*This*, and no other, was the original Gawain story'; but we may, I think, be able to specify certain incidents, saying, '*This* belongs to Gawain and to no other of King Arthur's knights. *That* adventure is a necessary and integral part of his story.'

One of the most striking characteristics of Gawain, and one which may undoubtedly be referred to the original conception of his character, is that of the waxing and waning of his strength as the day advances and declines. Probably the earliest version of this is the one given by Chrêtien's continuator, Gautier de Doulens:

> '*Hardemens et force doubloit*
> *Toustans puis ke midis passoit,*
> *Por voir, a monsignor Gauvain,*
> *Tout en devons estre certain;*
> *Quant la clartés del jor faloit*
> *Icelle force tresaloit*
> *Et de miedi en avant*
> *Li recroissoit tot autretant.*'[1]

[1] *Conte del Graal*, Potvin's edition, vol. iii. p. 334, vv. 19139-46.

EARLY CONCEPTIONS OF GAWAIN 13

The *Merlin* gives it somewhat differently, *e.g.* '*quant il se levoit au matin il avoit la force al millor chevalier del monde; et quant vint à eure de prime si li doubloit, et à eure de tierce ausi. et quant ce vint à eure de midi si revenoit à sa premiere force, ou il avoit esté au matin; et quant vint à eure de nonne et à toutes les eures de la nuit estoit il toudis en sa premiere force.*'[1]

Malory has again another version:[2] | '*but Sir Gawayne fro it passed 9 of the clok waxed ever stronger and stronger | for thenne hit cam to the hour of noone and thryes his myghte was encreaced. | And thenne whan it was past noone | and whan it drewe toward evensong Syre Gawayne's strengthe febled and waxt passynge faint that unnethe he myght dure ony lenger.*'

And later on:[3] '*Then had Syr Gawayne suche a grace and gyfte that an holy man had gyven to hym | That every day in the year from underne tyl hyghe noone hys myght encreaced tho thre houres as moche as thryse hys strengthe.*'

This, though the latest version, and ascribing a reason for the peculiarity utterly out of keeping with Gawain's general character in the romance (for he is certainly no favourite with 'holy men') agrees better with the *Perceval* than with the *Merlin*.

Scholars have seen in this growth and waning of Gawain's power, directly connected as it is with the waxing and waning of the sun, a proof that this Celtic hero was at one time a solar divinity.

Another characteristic of Gawain, in which he differs from the other knights, is that he possesses a steed, which

---

[1] *Roman de Merlin*, chap. xii. p. 137, Sommer's edition.
[2] *Morte d'Arthur*, Book iv. chap. 18, Sommer's edition.
[3] *Ibid.*, Book xx. chap. 21.

is known by a special name. *Gringalet*, or *le Gringalet*, is the form generally found in the French romances, but Professor Zimmer maintains that the name is more correctly *Gingalet* or *Guingalet*, a view to which the Welsh form of the word, *Keincaled*, lends support.[1] This horse figures repeatedly in the old romances; the *Merlin*[2] gives a long account of how Gawain at the outset of his knightly career won it by force of arms from the Saxon king, Clarions. There has been a great deal of discussion as to the original meaning of the name; the author of the *Merlin* says the steed was so called '*por sa grant bonté*'; Bartsch, commenting on the names given in the *Parzival*, gives as its meaning '*cheval maigre et alerte*'; Zimmer prefers '*schön-ausdauernd*' (as we should say, *of good staying power*); M. Gaston Paris more cautiously says that the name was originally Celtic, but that its signification has been lost.[3] In any case it doubtless referred to some special virtue in the steed, which, judging from the frequency with which it was stolen, or taken by stratagem, from its rightful owner, was a highly desirable possession.

One point which Zimmer brings out, in the article above referred to, is of special interest and significance in its bearing on the direction in which we must seek for light on the *earliest* forms of the Gawain story. The name of this horse, so closely connected with the hero, and that in romances admittedly belonging to an early stage of the Arthurian cycle, only occurs *once* in Welsh literature, and

[1] Cf. Zimmer on the Arthurian names, *Zeitschrift für Französische Sprache*, xiii.
[2] *Merlin*, chap. xxvii. pp. 363, 365.
[3] *Hist. Litt.*, xxx. pp. 36, 37, where M. Paris gives a list of the romances in which 'le Gringalet' figures.

EARLY CONCEPTIONS OF GAWAIN

then in a triad preserved in a late twelfth-century MS., where it is found in company with the horse of a certain Gilbert, identified by Zimmer as an Anglo-Norman follower of Henry I.[1] Even in stories of which we possess parallel versions, such for instance as the Erec (Geraint), which has come down to us in French, German, and Welsh, the *Welsh* writer refrains from mentioning Gawain's famous steed, where, in the parallel French passages, the name occurs. Zimmer opines that the omission was of set purpose, the name being a foreign one. Without entering into the question as to which of the versions, the French or the Welsh, is dependent on the other, it seems clear that the Northern French poets and romancers did not get the *Gringalet* tradition from *Wales*, yet the horse figures in stories which manifestly represent the oldest version we at present possess of Gawain's adventures. The inference seems to be that we must go *behind* the Welsh stories to arrive at the earliest form of the legend; that we need even pass through them on our journey to the remote Celtic antiquity in which the key to the main problem of our study will be found, seems increasingly doubtful.

It is practically certain that if Gawain were ever looked upon as a solar hero he would in that character have been possessed of a steed of especial beauty and value. Teutonic mythology is on this point very instructive. Siegfried's famous horse *Grani* was undoubtedly originally such a sun-horse. Odin and Freyr have each of them their own steed.

But besides the horse the 'solar' hero ought also to possess a sword, and in the early romances we find Gawain in possession of a sword, and that no other than *Excalibur*.

---

[1] This identification is however extremely problematic. See M. Ferd. Lot, *Romania*, xxiv.

16 THE LEGEND OF SIR GAWAIN

Chrêtien[1] mentions Escalibur as Gawain's sword without any comment, but as if his possession of it were a well-known fact. In the *Merlin*[2] we have an account of how Arthur, on the occasion of bestowing knighthood on his nephew, presented him with Escalibur; and Gawain throughout the romance wields that weapon, Arthur having the sword he won from the giant king, Rion. Sir F. Madden, in his 'Introduction,' says that Arthur *lent* the sword to his nephew, an error into which he probably fell by yielding to the preconceived idea that Escalibur could belong to no one but Arthur. But there is no trace of a *loan* in the *Merlin*; it is a permanent *gift*.

Here, Escalibur is not the sword given by the mysterious Lady of the Lake, but that fixed in the block of stone, which Arthur alone can withdraw, thereby proving his right to the kingdom—an adventure attributed in the *Queste* to Galahad, and which probably finds its earliest form in the famous sword of the Branstock, which, as we know, was a divine weapon.

A peculiarity of Escalibur, mentioned in the *Merlin*, is that it throws so great a light when drawn that it is as if two torches had been kindled—a peculiarity distinctly suggestive of a 'sun' weapon.[3] Professor Zimmer[4] identifies this sword *Caliburnus* (Latin), *Escalibor* (French), *Caledvwlch* (Welsh), with *Caladbolg*, the great sword of the early Irish, or Ultonian, cycle. This sword was forged in Fairyland, and when drawn from the sheath 'waxed greater than the rainbow,'—a somewhat curious simile, which

---
[1] *Conte del Graal*, vol. ii. line 7280.
[2] *Merlin*, chap. xxi. p. 270.
[3] *Ibid.*, chap. vii. p. 99.
[4] Zimmer, *Gott. Gelehrte Anz.*, 1890, No. xii. pp. 516-17.

though doubtless understood by the chronicler as referring simply to the far-reaching sweep of the weapon, yet may not improbably indicate some original 'light-giving' quality, analogous to that mentioned above of Escalibur.

Students of the legend will remember that there is a decided confusion as to the sword which Arthur wields: it is sometimes that drawn from the stone, sometimes that won from King Rion, sometimes the gift of the Lady of the Lake; the name Escalibor (Excalibur) is given both to the first and last named of these weapons. Judging from analogy, the sword of the stone, which finds its parallel in early Northern saga, should be the original sword of the story, and the only one to which a really divine origin can justly be ascribed. It is *this* sword, and not either of the other two, which Arthur gives to Gawain.

The fact that the weapon can also be traced back to early Irish legend in no way militates against the suggestion that Gawain may have been, in Arthurian legend, its original possessor; quite the contrary. We shall find in the progress of this investigation that between Gawain, and the great hero of the Ultonian cycle, Cuchulinn, there exist many striking parallels. There is probably no hero of the Arthurian cycle, not excepting Arthur himself, who stands in so close a relation to the heroes of early Irish legend, or presents so many points of contact with their stories as the gallant nephew of the British king.

We shall scarcely go far astray if we believe that Gawain, at the outset of his career, was equipped as befitted a 'solar' hero, with a steed and sword of exceptional virtue; nor shall we, I believe, be wrong if we accept the statement of the early romance-writers and believe that the sword was *Excalibur*.

CHAPTER III

THE LEGEND IN CHRÉTIEN'S 'CONTE DEL GRAAL' AND WOLFRAM'S 'PARZIVAL'

Summary of the two poems—Wolfram's conclusion probably independent and genuine.

HAVING thus, as far as possible, ascertained what was the primitive conception of Gawain in the Celtic mind, we will endeavour to discover what were the details of the story connected with him. The task is a difficult one, but it may be simplified if we take, as basis for our inquiry, that Romance which is now generally considered to be the earliest of the Gawain cycle, and in which his adventures are related in the clearest and most coherent manner—the *Perceval*, or *Conte del Graal* of Chrétien de Troyes. I have also coupled with Chrétien's poem at the heading of this chapter the *Parzival* of Wolfram von Eschenbach. The source of this poem is undoubtedly closely related to that of Chrétien, and it also gives the conclusion of Gawain's adventures, which Chrétien, who left his work unfinished, was unable to do.

I would guard against being supposed to hold that the version of these two poets represents the *original* Gawain legend, but by taking this as a basis of comparison, and ascertaining which of the incidents there related figure most persistently in other romances of the cycle, we may be assisted in arriving at a conclusion as to the character of the fundamental *données* of the story.

In both poems, that of Chrêtien and of Wolfram, the ostensible hero of the Romance is Perceval, but a large proportion, practically half of the entire work, is dedicated to the adventures of Gawain. These adventures are kept distinct from those of the original hero (though Wolfram, at least, is careful never to lose sight entirely of Parzival) and are far simpler and less complicated than is the case with other 'Gawain' romances.

In both poems Gawain makes his first appearance on the scene in connection with the love-trance into which Perceval is plunged by the sight of the blood-drops on the snow, a trance which keeps him motionless and unconscious in close proximity to Arthur's camp. It is Gawain who breaks the spell by covering the blood-stains, and after revealing his name to Perceval conducts him to the presence of the king. During the subsequent feast held in Perceval's honour, the loathly messenger of the Grail appears and curses Perceval for his failure to ask the question at the Grail Castle; she also tells of the imprisoned queens in the Château-Merveil, and, in Chrêtien, of other adventures of which no more is heard, and which therefore need not be specified here. Immediately on her departure, the knight, Guingambrésil (Chrétien) or Kingrimursel (Wolfram) arrives on the scene, and accusing Gawain of having treacherously murdered his lord, challenges him to single combat, and fixes the place and time of their meeting. The feast breaks up in disorder, and the two heroes ride forth on their respective quests.

Gawain's first adventure, which is related with much

more charm and felicity by the German than by the French[1] poet, is to aid an old knight whose castle is besieged by the rejected lover of his elder daughter. Gawain takes part in the tournament as the chosen knight of the younger, a mere child, and by his valour determines the fortunes of the day in favour of his side. Leaving the castle, Gawain rides to Escavalon, or Askalon, the scene of the proposed combat, where he is met by the king of the land, who, ignorant of his identity, sends him to his castle, commending him to the care of his sister.

The lady proves to be of surpassing beauty, and Gawain makes overtures of love, to which she readily responds. They are interrupted by an old knight, who recognises Gawain as the supposed murderer of his master, and incites the inhabitants of the city to attack him. Gawain and the lady take refuge in a tower, and defend themselves with a chessboard and the stone pieces belonging to it. The king returns in company with Guingambrésil, by whose representations the strife is ended, the single combat deferred for a year, and Gawain allowed to depart in safety, having undertaken in the meanwhile to ride in search of either the Bleeding Lance of the Grail Castle (Chrêtien), or the Grail itself (Wolfram).

Gawain next falls in with a maiden and a wounded knight, whom he assists and is warned by them of the dangers of the way. He, however, continues, and soon meets a lady of dazzling beauty, sitting beside a spring of water. Gawain makes advances to her, to which she replies with scant courtesy, but tells him if he will fetch her

[1] A third version to be found in *Diu Krône* of H. von dem Türlin, who knows both Chrêtien and Wolfram, but follows the former the more closely.

horse from a garden near at hand she will ride with him. The knight does this, and is again warned by the dwellers in the garden of the maiden's evil designs.

They ride off together, followed at a distance by a hideous dwarf, according to Wolfram, the lady's attendant.

Reaching the wounded knight, Gawain dismounts to bind his wounds, when the former, by a *ruse*, gains possession of Gawain's horse, and rides off, thus forcing Gawain either to go on foot or to mount the wretched steed belonging to the dwarf. The lady mocks him continuously, and, on their arrival at a meadow bounded by water, on the farther side of which is seen a magnificent castle, deserts him, and is ferried over the water by a boatman, while Gawain is attacked by a knight mounted on his (Gawain's) steed, *le Gringalet*. The hero overthrows him, on which the boatman appears, and claims the steed of the vanquished knight as his toll. Gawain represents that the horse is, in truth, his own, and offers the rider in exchange. They cross the water, and Gawain is courteously entertained for the night by the boatman.

In the morning the hero is attracted by the appearance of the castle, at the windows of which he sees many richly-dressed ladies. His host endeavours to dissuade him from attempting the adventure of the castle, which is enchanted, '*Le Château Merveil*'; but Gawain persists, enters the building, and seats himself on a wonderful couch, the '*Lit merveil*.' He is immediately assailed by invisible foes with a storm of stones, and bolts shot from the crossbow; and, having successfully withstood these assaults, by a furious lion, which he slays.

The enchantments of the castle are now at an end. The inhabitants acclaim Gawain as their lord, and he is presented to the queens of the castle, three in number (according to Wolfram, *four*), one old and white-haired, the others respectively her daughter and granddaughter. The old queen is in reality Arthur's mother, who has either eloped with, or been carried off by, the magician who built the castle; the other two, mother and sister to Gawain himself, but neither side is aware of the relationship.

A curious trait occurs at this point in Chrêtien's version. The boatman tells Gawain that whoever achieves the adventure of the castle must remain there; '*que jamais de cette maison n'istroit u fust tors u raison*,'[1] at which Gawain is exceedingly angry; but nothing comes of the prohibition. In both poems he leaves the castle the following morning to fight with a knight whom the lady who had accompanied him to the castle brings to oppose him.

Gawain vanquishes this knight, all the ladies of the castle looking on at the combat, and then with the lady of his choice (*l'Orgueilleuse de Logres* in Chrêtien; *Orgeluse* in Wolfram), who is still contemptuous, rides on a further quest—to weave a garland from the flowers, or pluck the bough of a tree, guarded by Guiromelans or Gramoflanz. To do this Gawain has to brave the adventure of the 'Perilous Ford' (crossing a river which flows through a rocky ravine), which he does successfully, wins his garland, is challenged by Guiromelans to single combat, and learns from him the rank and identity of the queens of the Château Merveil. On his return to the 'Proud Lady' she receives him kindly, and apologises for her former contemptuous conduct, which was simply meant to spur him on to avenge her wrongs upon Guiromelans, who had slain her lover.

[1] Cf. *Conte del Graal*, vol. iii. verses 9393 *et seq.*

CHRÊTIEN AND WOLFRAM

They return to the castle, where Gawain is received with great honour. He sends a messenger to Arthur to invite him to assist with all his court at the approaching conflict between the hero and Guiromelans. The messenger finds the court plunged in grief at Gawain's supposed death.

Here Chrêtien's version breaks off abruptly, but the story is continued, as follows, by Wolfram:—

Arthur and Guinevere eagerly promise to go to the trysting-place named by Gawain, and the messenger returns with the news. Gawain weds Orgeluse (the connection between the two is somewhat vague in Chrêtien), and so soon as Arthur's court has been seen to pass on the farther side of the water, follows them. He makes all the ladies whom he has freed from captivity draw rein in a ring round the tent of King Arthur, a display which excites Kay's wrath and envy,

'*Got mit den liuten wunder tuot,*
Wer gap Gâwân die frouwen luot?'[1]

The next morning Gawain, riding forth to prove if he be sufficiently recovered from the wounds received at the Château Merveil, meets Parzival; neither recognises the other, and a fierce conflict ensues in which Gawain is worsted, and would be slain, save that his pages, passing at the critical moment, call upon him by name, and Parzival, learning that his opponent is his friend and kinsman, throws away his sword. The single combat between Gawain and Gramoflanz is deferred for another day, and finally, by the efforts of King Arthur and Brandelidelein, Gramoflanz's

---

[1] Cf. *Parzival,* Bk. xiii. verses 1454-55:
'*God worketh with some His wonders,*
Who gave Gawain this woman-folk?'

uncle, prevented altogether; Gramoflanz wedding Gawain's sister, whose love he had won while she was imprisoned in the Château Merveil.

Gawain's adventures are now completed, and he retires into the background, the remaining books of the poem being devoted to the principal hero, Parzival.

It has been supposed by critics that the latter part of Wolfram's poem, as well as the first two books, which are also independent of Chrêtien, was the invention of the German poet, but I shall hope to show, in the progress of these Studies, that incidents parallel to those related in Wolfram are to be found elsewhere; and even in the portion which he shares in common with Chrêtien there is at least one important incident of which the French poet knows nothing, but which is preserved in an independent romance.

Critics have also objected that the Grail quest, undertaken by Gawain, is allowed to drop into oblivion, and that this must be owing to the fact that Chrêtien left his poem unfinished. Had he completed it, he would, they say, have brought Gawain, as well as Perceval, to the Grail castle; and Wolfram, taking Chrêtien for his guide, would have done the same, instead of leaving Gawain, as he does, simply lord of the Château Merveil, and its bevy of fair ladies.

But this is, I believe, an entirely mistaken view. When the Gawain adventures are examined in the light of earlier parallels, it will, I think, become apparent that it is exactly at this point that the story *should* end; that the Grail quest is entirely independent of Gawain, and its introduction due to the growing popularity of this feature of the Arthurian cycle, a popularity which eventually issued in sending *all* the knights of the Round Table, without distinction, in search of the Grail.

It will follow from this that we shall find that the German poet was not giving reins to his fancy, but following a genuine tradition, identical in source, though varying in detail, with that followed by Chrêtien.

CHAPTER IV

THE LEGEND IN THE MINOR ROMANCES

General character of the incidents most frequently alluded to—List of such incidents—The romances in which they occur—Parallel with Cuchulinn's adventures in *The Wooing of Emer*.

HAVING now laid the basis for our inquiry, we will proceed to compare the version given by other romances with that which we have chosen as our point of comparison. It may of course be objected that, owing to the widespread popularity of Chrêtien's poems, the recurrence of adventures related by him can prove nothing more than that the writers of the later romances knew Chrêtien This is to some extent true, but if the popularity of Chrêtien alone were the operating cause we should expect to find that the writers made either a general choice among the adventures related by him, or that they gave the preference to those which showed Gawain in the most chivalrous light, such, for instance, as the charming episode of his acting as the little maiden's knight. This, as told by Wolfram especially, is certainly the most graceful and poetical episode connected with Gawain.

But this is not the case. We find that, as a rule, the incidents parallel with Chrêtien's poem belong to the final stages of the Gawain adventures, *i.e.* they represent the *marvellous* rather than the *knightly* and *chivalrous* feats of the hero.

Thus, neither the tournament episode, nor the adventure with the king of Escavalon's sister, meet us as often as do the following: the theft of Gawain's horse; his crossing the water to achieve a special quest; his connection with a lady of supernatural origin, queen or mistress of a magic castle or island;[1] and the fact of his supposed death.

It would therefore appear that some reason other than Chrêtien's popularity has been at work to determine this selection. May it not have been that there was a floating, half-forgotten tradition of the primitive Gawain story, which pointed out these episodes as having, at some far back period, formed part of the original feats of the hero? As we shall see, there exist parallels in Celtic myth and literature which seem to argue a very early basis for such stories.

It may be well here to mention some of the romances which contain incidents similar to those named above; to some of which it will not be necessary to refer at length later on. The small incident of the theft of Gawain's horse is found both in the *Vengeance de Raguidel*[2] and the *Cimétière Perilleux*.[3] In a note on p. 14 reference has already been made to the list given by M. Gaston Paris of romances in which *Le Gringalet* figures by name. In *Rigomer*,[4] in *Guinglain*[5] or *Le Bel Inconnu*, in *Saigremor*,[6] in *Diu*

[1] In the German poem the connection of the Lady Orgeluse with the magic castle is much closer than in Chrêtien. On this point see next chapter.

[2] Cf. abstract given in *Hist. Litt. de la France*, vol. xxx. p. 54.

[3] Cf. *Hist. Litt.*, p. 80.   [4] *Ibid.*, p. 91.

[5] *Ibid.*, p. 176.   [6] *Ibid.*, p. 262.

Krône, and in English romances such as *The Marriage of Sir Gawayne*,[1] and one version of *The Carle of Carlile*, we find Gawain closely connected with a lady, who is either herself a fairy or the near relation of a magician; while the *Demoiselle du Gautdestroit* or *l'Orgeilleuse pucelle* figures frequently. References to an adventure, either on an island, or at a castle which can only be reached by crossing the water, occur in *Le Chevalier de la Charrette*,[2] in *Perceval li Gallois*[3] (prose), *Diu Krône*, *Vengeance de Raguidel* (a morass), *Gauvain et l'Échiquier*;[4] *Méraugis de Port les gues*,[5] and *Saigremor*; while the prologue to Book xiv. of the *Reductorium Morale*[6] of Pierre Bercheur (who died about 1362) gives a curious adventure of Gawain's in a palace *under* the water.

The incident of Gawain's supposed death is treated at great length in *Diu Krône*; and also occurs in *Le Cimétière Perilleux*, in *Mériaduc*,[7] and in the prose *Perceval*.

Mr. Alfred Nutt, in a note to the English translation of the *Parzival* (vol. ii. Book x.), points out that Irish literature presents a parallel to the whole of the *Gawain-Proud-Lady* episode in the wooing of Emer by Cuchulinn —a hero with whom, as we shall eventually see, Gawain otherwise comes into close connection.

This story, which has been translated in full by Professor

---

[1] The English romances are given in Sir Frederick Madden's collection, *Sir Gawayne*.

[2] An analysis and study of this romance have been given by M. Gaston Paris, *Romania* xii. It will be referred to fully later on.

[3] Potvin's edition of the *Perceval*, vol. i.

[4] *Hist. Litt.*, xxx. p. 82.   [5] *Ibid.*, p. 226.

[6] Introduction to Madden's *Sir Gawayne*, p. xxxii.

[7] *Hist. Litt.*, p. 241.

Kuno Meyer,[1] runs, briefly summarised, as follows:—Cuchulinn, the nephew of Conchobar, king of Ulster, being pressed to marry, rejects all the damsels suggested to him, and determines to wed Emer, the daughter of Forgall the Wily. He visits the maiden in person, but, though fascinated by his beauty, she declines to listen to his wooing, scornfully characterising the feats of which he boasts as '*goodly fights of a tender boy*.' She will not yield to him till he has fulfilled certain conditions, and proved himself a valiant warrior. Forgall, who is a master of magic arts, and does not desire his daughter to wed Cuchulinn, goes in disguise to Conchobar's court, and persuades the king to send his nephew to Scathach (who seems to be a mixture of the Wise Woman and the Amazon) to learn feats of arms. Cuchulinn sets forth and has to face many dangers, the first, a beast like a lion, which, however, does not harm him, and the 'foul play of the youths who mocked at him.' Then he must cross the *Plain of Ill-luck*, which he does by the aid of a wheel and an apple, which he throws before him, following in the track thus made. He traverses the *Perilous Glen*, and eventually reaches the dwelling of Scathach, which is beyond the water, by means of a dangerous bridge, which rises and throws the hero back when he attempts to cross. Having achieved all these feats, and learnt all Scathach can teach him, he returns, an accomplished warrior, to wed the lady of his choice.

It will hardly be denied that a general resemblance between this story and the Gawain-Proud-Lady episode exists.

---

[1] Cf. *Archaeological Review*, 1888, Nos. 1-4, for the vulgate text, which probably represents an eleventh-century redaction, and *Revue Celtique*, vol. xiii., for the short text, which Professor Kuno Meyer assigns to the eighth century.

For our purpose there are two points which should be especially noted: (*a*) that the maiden is closely connected with a magician; (*b*) that these incidents do *not* occur in the Welsh *Peredur*, which offers so close a parallel to the *Perceval* section of the story. To both of these points we shall return shortly.

As during the progress of these Studies we shall frequently have occasion to refer to Cuchulinn, it may be well here to say something on the subject of that hero, the leading figure of the early Irish or Ultonian heroic cycle. Whether or not the personages of this cycle had any historical existence it is not easy to say. They are regarded as having lived in the decades immediately preceding and following the birth of Christ, and the legends relating to them had been woven into stories and fixed in writing by the seventh century.[1]

In this early Irish tradition the court of Conchobar, king of Ulster, is represented, like that of Arthur, as the rallying-point for the heroes of his day. Research has not yet decisively determined the source and origin of the Round Table, but there is a very general opinion among scholars that in the circumstances of Conchobar's court we have one of the earliest parallels to that famous mediæval institution.

Cuchulinn, whose glory overshadowed that of Conchobar, was the king's nephew, being son of Dechtire, Conchobar's sister, and Lug the Light-god, afterwards looked upon as Lord of the Other-world. Thus his relation to Conchobar exactly parallels that of Gawain to Arthur, and the elementary connection thus established will be found to extend to other points, some of them striking in their correspondence.

[1] Cf. Zimmer, *Keltische Studien*, v.

THE LEGEND IN MINOR ROMANCES

For the present chapter it is enough to remark that the Cuchulinn-Emer parallel practically covers all the latter part of the story as told by Chrêtien and Wolfram, and appears to afford an assurance that we shall not go wrong in selecting this portion of Gawain's adventures as reflecting most closely the original form of the story, and therefore as being the point to which we must direct our special investigation.

CHAPTER V

THE MAGIC CASTLE

*The Castle in Chrêtien and Wolfram—Castles regarded as other-world dwellings—The lady and the magician—The Isle of Women—*Diu Krône*—The Voyage of Bran*—Death of Gawain, real and supposed—Gawain in Fairyland—Apparition of Gawain to Arthur—Real significance of the Château Merveil adventure—Visit to the otherworld in Teutonic and Celtic mythology—Position of this adventure in the Gawain legend.

THE short summary of the preceding chapter has shown us clearly that one of the adventures most generally attributed to Gawain is the winning of a castle, or kingdom, only to be approached by water. The form varies, but the attribution of some mysterious water-adventure to this hero is remarkably frequent.

As given by Chrêtien and Wolfram it may be summarised as follows:—Gawain approaches the castle under the conduct of a lady whom he has met under mysterious circumstances; the fact that she is found seated beside a spring or fountain is indicative of her unearthly origin. The castle is, so far as we can gather, on an island; apparently it can only be approached, or quitted, by water, and Chrêtien in particular emphasises the fact that the water is so wide that no engine of war could throw a missile across it.

THE MAGIC CASTLE

> *'Et s'est lée c'on une fronde*
> *de mangonel ne de perrière*
> *ne jetast outre la rivière*
> *ne arbalestres n'i transist.'*[1]

This castle is inhabited by three (or four) queens, and a crowd of maidens, four hundred according to Wolfram; Chrêtien does not enumerate the ladies, but gives the number of knights as five hundred—probably the maidens equalled them. But Wolfram gives us most clearly to understand that, though dwellers in the same castle, knights and ladies had nothing to do with each other— an important point as determining the real nature of the castle; thus,

> *'Sie wârn ein ander unbekant,*
> *unt beslôz se doch ein porte,*
> *daz sie ze gegenworte*
> *nie kômen, frouwen noch die man.'*[2]

What is the exact connection between the lady who has guided Gawain and the castle it is not very easy to discover, but it is much closer in the *German* than in the *French* poem. In the former she has concluded an alliance with the magician who owns the castle, and is evidently regarded with the greatest respect by the dwellers within it. She is fairer than any of the captive maidens; and it is she, rather than the old queen, who seems to be looked upon as its mistress.

Chrêtien, as we have seen, also tells us that he who wins

---

[1] *Conte del Graal,* vol. ii. verses 8588-91.
[2] '*Unknown were they yet to each other, tho' one portal it shut them in,*
And never a man nor a maiden might speech of each other win.'
  Parzival, Book xiii. 320-23.

the castle must remain there for the rest of his life; a prohibition which evidently belonged to an earlier form of the story, and the significance of which has become obscured, as Gawain pays no attention to it. To sum up: Chrêtien's and Wolfram's Castle is on an island, inhabited by women, keeping themselves apart from men, and owning as mistress a lady of surpassing beauty. To win this Island Castle involves permanent residence there.

Now it is well known that ancient mythology, both Celtic and Teutonic, represented the abode of the dead sometimes as an *Island* (such as the Isle of Avalon), sometimes as a *Castle* (such as the castle inhabited by Brynhild in the *Thidrek-saga* and *Nibelungenlied*[1]). The lot of the dwellers in such an other-world was no unhappy one; their surroundings were fair, even luxurious; the one drawback was that they were unable to leave the place of their imprisonment. This latter feature is strongly brought out in the speech of the old queen to Gawain (*Parzival* xiii. 949-1020). The passage is too long to quote in its entirety, but she begins by telling the hero how Klingsor has built the castle which he (Gawain) has now won, imprisoning in it all whom he makes captive, Christian or heathen. She beseeches Gawain to set them all free, as residence in a strange land is a grief to her:

> '*Swaz er gesach der werden*
> *ûf Kristenlîcher erden,*
> *ez waere mâget wîb oder man,*
> *der ist in hie vil undertân:*
> *manc heide unde heidenîn*
> *muost' ouch bî uns hie ûffe sîn.*

---

[1] Cf. *Legends of the Wagner Drama—Siegfried*,—where I have discussed this question at greater length.

*nu lât daz volc wider komen
da nâch uns sorge si vernomen.
ellende frumt mir'z herze kalt.'*[1]

She then illustrates her meaning by a quaint riddling parallel of ice born of water and turning to water again, as joy is succeeded by sorrow, and that again turns to joy. Finally, after alluding to the welcome they will receive on their return she concludes with the suggestive words:

*' Hêrre ich hân lange hie gebiten:
nie geloufen noch geriten
kom her der mich erkande,
Der mir sorgen wande.'*[2]

There is no doubt here that the queen's residence in the Magic Castle is an unwilling one.

If the poems be compared it will be found that this idea is much more clearly brought out in the *German* than in the *French* version. True, the passage just quoted occurs *after* the point at which Chrêtien's share in the story abruptly closes, so we have comparatively little material for determining the light in which he really regarded the castle. The account given to Gawain by the boatman seems to indicate that it was really the property

---

[1] 'And all who from Christian countries 'neath the spell of his magic lay,
Be they woman, or man, or maiden, are thy vassals both one and all,
And many from lands of paynim with us 'neath his power must fall.
Let this folk then now get them homewards, where yet for our loss they mourn,
For to dwell in the land of the stranger, it maketh my heart forlorn.'
   Parzival, English translation, vol. ii. p. 89.

[2] 'Sir Knight, here o'er long I stay,
Yet there cometh no man who doth know me and turneth my care away.'   *Ibid.*, ii. p. 90.

of the elder queen, having been erected with the treasure she brought into the land. The architect of the castle '*I sages clers d'astrenomie*' plays no part in the story, and is certainly never regarded as its lord—a fact of importance in deciding the relative connection of these two poems.

As was hinted in the last chapter, and as we shall find clearly brought out when we discuss the personality of Gawain's love, that lady is closely connected with a magician, or a prince possessed of magic powers. Probably she was originally his *daughter*. In *Diu Krône*, a poem to which we shall have occasion to refer frequently, she is his *niece*, and he is undoubtedly the owner and master of the castle.

The fact that Chrêtien has altogether dropped the magician, while Wolfram retains him, and though never bringing him personally on the stage (which in accordance with the original form of the story he doubtless ought to have done) yet preserves his close connection with the castle, and in a lesser degree with the lady, goes far to prove that the German poet was independent of the French, and drew his account, preserving an archaic feature Chrêtien had dropped, from another source. That he *invented* a situation so consonant with primitive tradition is hardly likely.

But to return to the character of the castle:—Scholars are now pretty generally agreed on the point that Gawain's castle *does* represent such an other-world dwelling; and when we turn to Celtic mythology the real nature of the adventure becomes clearly apparent.

Part of the old Irish paradise was known as the '*Isle of Women*,' and was inhabited exclusively by women, ruled over by a queen of unearthly beauty, who is represented as occasionally visiting the earth, and inviting a chosen hero to return with her to her kingdom. We find an account of such a visit in the *Voyage of Bran*,[1] and a similar tale is told of Connla,[2] son of Cond, and of Oisin.[3]

Gawain, even as these heroes, reaches his wonder-castle under the guidance of its fair mistress; and a feature recurring in the Irish tales, the bearing of a branch of a wondrous tree by the queen, seems reflected in the command laid upon the knight to pluck the bough of the tree guarded by Gramoflanz. The direction given in Chrétien, to pluck *any* of the flowers which he sees, is much less significant.

In *Diu Krône* of Heinrich von dem Türlin, a most curious compilation of adventures of which Gawain is the chief hero, we find it related that he reaches in a mysterious manner, apparently on a floating islet, a land where no man dwells, but maidens only, ruled over by a queen, '*Der Meide-land*.' This lady offers Gawain his choice between becoming her consort, and remaining in the land, or receiving the balsam of eternal youth as a gift ere he leaves the island. Gawain chooses the latter.[4] We do not know the sources of this curious poem; Heinrich certainly knew both Chrétien and Wolfram, but he adds many adventures, some of a curiously archaic character, unknown to either of these writers.

In the light of this testimony it becomes evident that Gawain's adventure was not merely a visit to the other-world, but specifically to the other-world as conceived of

---

[1] *Voyage of Bran*, by Prof. Kuno Meyer and Alfred Nutt.
[2] *Ibid.*, p. 144; also appendix to *Tannhauser—Legends of the Wagner Drama*. [3] *Ibid.*, p. 149.
[4] *Diu Krône*, 17329 *et seq.*

in Celtic mythology. Nor would such an adventure be out of keeping with the original conception of Gawain as a solar hero, as comparison with the Siegfried myth will prove. The original consequences of such a visit would be that the hero would be unable to return to the upper world, though under certain circumstances, which will be pointed out later, these consequences are waived.

Here the passage quoted from Chrêtien (p. 22) as to the impossibility of the achiever of the venture leaving the castle, becomes very important as a witness to the original nature of the adventure. *The Voyage of Bran* shows us clearly what would be the result, as a rule, of an attempt to return to the earth. Bran and his companions depart from the Magic Isles, but are warned, if they return to Ireland, not to set foot on shore. One of the band disobeys the injunction, and immediately falls to ashes '*as if he had been in the earth for many hundred years*'[1]—in plain words, he and his companions had long been dead.

This is, I believe, the true explanation of the many references to Gawain's death, real or supposed, in the Romances, references not to be paralleled in the case of any of the other knights. Tristan dies, of course, but his death has but little effect on the cycle. Lancelot outlives Arthur; Perceval's death is but vaguely referred to, but there is no doubt as to the death of Gawain, and the grief caused by his loss. Further, this death is, over and over again, foreshadowed by Gawain's disappearance from the Court, when the rumour gains ground that he has been slain. The original Gawain had passed to the land from whence there was no return, and, in spite of the glamour surrounding his dwelling, the fact that he was in reality dead

[1] *Voyage of Bran*, p. 32.

was impressed firmly upon the minds of those who first told his story, and in one shape or another it has coloured that story ever since.

That tradition to the effect that Gawain was still living, but in Fairyland, was current in the Middle Ages, is evident from quotations given by Sir F. Madden in the Introduction to his *Sir Gawayne*.[1] The first, which is from the *Roman de Guillaume d'Orange*, represents King Arthur as receiving Renouart in Fairyland, and pointing out to him the heroes who are his companions, among them Roland, Iwein, and Gawain. Another quotation, from Chaucer, speaks of

> '*Sir Gawayne with his old curtesie,*
> *Tho' he come again out of Fairie*
> *He could him nought amendin in no worde.*'

As indications of this tradition we may cite *Saigremor*,[2] where Gawain is kept a prisoner in the Isle of the fairy Karmente; and *Meraugis de Port les guez*,[3] where he is again the prisoner of a lady on an island, and forced to combat all comers. He will not be freed till he himself is overcome. This last adventure, which is in Malory attributed to *Balan*, seems, from the fact that the conflict is watched by ladies within the castle, to have been originally closely connected, if not identical, with the Château Merveil episode.

Malory[4] has a curious account of the apparition of Gawain's ghost, surrounded by a bevy of fair ladies, to King Arthur. Malory explains his companions as being the spirits of those for whom Gawain had fought while

---

[1] Introduction, p. xxxvi.
[2] *Hist. Litt.*, xxx. p. 262.
[3] *Ibid.*, p. 226.
[4] *Morte d'Arthur*, Book xxi. chap. iii.

40 THE LEGEND OF SIR GAWAIN

alive. Dr. Sommer considers that one source of this twenty-first book was a romance analogous to, but not identical with, the prose *Lancelot*. There, Gawain's ghost appears surrounded by 'many poor people,' who tell Arthur they have helped Gawain to conquer the heavenly kingdom[1]—a version far too edifying to be the original one.

It seems possible that the account given by Wolfram of Gawain's return from the Château Merveil,[2] accompanied by a party of fair ladies, with whom he surrounds Arthur's tent, is directly, or indirectly, at the root of this incident. No other romance which I have examined contains anything at all resembling the episode, and it seems highly improbable, in the face of so curious a correspondence as that between Malory and the *Parzival*, that Wolfram invented the incident. He most probably found it in his French source, and it has been preserved by independent tradition.

Taking all these facts into consideration, we may, I think, hold it proved that a visit of Gawain to the other-world, here represented most closely by the Celtic *Isle of Women*, was an early, probably an *original*, part of the tradition connected with that hero. It is this tradition which lies at the basis of Chrêtien's and Wolfram's poems.

This admitted, what position should such a visit hold in the legend? It would in all probability be the hero's concluding feat. Certainly the earliest idea connected with such an expedition is, that it necessitated the hero remaining in the mysterious other-world, did he once succeed in reaching it. There are of course exceptions, but these seem to depend on the *motif* of the expedition—*i.e.* if it be

---

[1] Sommer, *On the Sources of Malory*, p. 266.
[2] Cf. quotation, p. 13.

undertaken unsolicited by the queen of the land, and with the view of releasing one there held in durance.

This feature seems to have been specially perpetuated in Northern mythology, where we have the expeditions of Hermodur, of Swipdag, and of Sigurd—all governed by what may be called the 'deliverance' *motif*.

But it is otherwise in the cases in which the hero responds to the invitation of the queen, and departs, rather under the exigence of a spell laid upon him, than in order to fulfil a task. This version seems to predominate in Celtic mythology; we have the cases mentioned above of Bran, Connla, and Oisin; and the story of Thomas the Rhymer would fall under the same heading. We have of course instances on either side of the operation of the other *motif*. The episode of Melwas or Méleagaunt, which we shall discuss later, seems to be a Celtic instance of the 'rescue' expedition, just as in German legend the Tannhäuser story corresponds to the 'invitation' form; but the general character of such legends seems to differ in the two mythologies in the manner indicated above.

Was the 'invitation' form the earlier? If so, this might help to explain some of the inconsistencies in the Gawain story—*i.e.* he first went at the invitation of the queen, and would thus be regarded as *par force* remaining in her land. Later on he was regarded as the rescuer of the ladies imprisoned in the Château Merveil, and in this character was enabled to return.

If this earlier form of the story were as we suppose— indeed, if the visit to the Château Merveil be in any way an original part of the Gawain legend,—then it is more than probable that the ending, as given by Wolfram, was no invention of the German poet, but based upon existing, if already somewhat involved, tradition. Had Chrétien lived to finish his poem, he would, I believe, have completed the Gawain episode in much the same manner—*i.e.* he would have left Gawain lord and master of the Château Merveil, as Perceval was of the Grail Castle.

And if we grant this, we should, I think, go a step further and admit that Gawain was not originally a 'Grail' hero at all, that that famous quest was no part of his own story, but has affected it through his connection with Perceval. That the 'Grail' castle as described in the Romances has certain other-world features is true, but these features are combined with others belonging to what Mr. Nutt in his 'Studies' designates as the '*Feud*' quest; and in the earliest forms of the story these latter features, as connected with what was apparently the original talisman, the Bleeding Lance, probably predominated.

It is worthy of note that the most striking ' other-world ' feature ever attributed to the Grail castle is found in connection precisely with that hero whose quest, there is reason to believe, *was* originally of such an other-world nature, *i.e.* with Gawain and not with Perceval. In *Diu Krône* it is the former who achieves the famous venture, which Perceval, by his neglect to ask the question, has failed in; and immediately on Gawain's uttering the mystic words, the old king joyfully informs him that, though apparently living, he and his companions are already dead, but compelled to preserve the semblance of life till the asking of the question breaks the spell. Having said this, he and all the knights who crowd the hall vanish, and Gawain and the Grail-bearer with her attendant maidens are left, the only living creatures in this veritable 'Castle of the Dead.'[1]

[1] Cf. *Diu Krône*, verses 29182-29619.

THE MAGIC CASTLE 43

Was the 'other-world' quest so closely connected with Gawain that it coloured all the stories into which he was brought? It would almost seem so. Certainly if there be one hero of all Arthur's Court who is connected with the world of the departed, either in the fantastic fairyland form in which ancient mythology clothed it, or in its sombre reality by pseudo-historical tradition relating to his death and place of burial—to say nothing of the many false reports of his decease—that hero is Gawain.

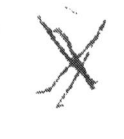

CHAPTER VI

THE LOVES OF GAWAIN

No special lady connected with Gawain—Conflicting testimony on the point—Gawain's character affected by the 'Castle' adventure—His love a supernatural maiden—Her connection with a magician—*Diu Krône*—Cuchulinn—This feature preserved in English romances—*The Marriage of Syr Gawayne*—Interesting Irish parallel—The Loathly Messenger—*The Carle of Carlile*—Summary of evidence—Its bearing on the question of transmission of the Arthurian legend.

IF we accept the conclusion arrived at in the preceding chapter, that Gawain's quest was originally of the nature of a visit to the other-world, and that in a form most consonant with Celtic myth, we should naturally expect to find some surviving traces of his connection with the queen of this other-world.

Of all the knights of King Arthur's Court, Gawain is certainly the one whose love-affairs, if we accept later tradition, we should expect to find, from the first, the most numerous and the least edifying. On the contrary, tradition on this point is curiously vague and incomplete. In all Gawain's story there is no trace of a *liaison* under circumstances of deception and treachery, such as is attributed to Lancelot or Tristan. How he came to win the reputation of a faithless libertine, such as later tradition represents him, it would be impossible, regarding his story merely on the surface, to say. M. Gaston Paris[1] points out that the name of no special lady is associated with his, as that of Enid is with Erec, or Guinevere and Iseult with the two heroes just mentioned. Gawain is rather the courteous and disinterested champion of *all* maidens than the lover of *one*. This vagueness of tradition, coupled with the hero's reputation as a model of chivalry, led in later romances to the association of his name, now with one, now with another; the same romance (as e.g. *Diu Krône*) sometimes crediting him with two distinct lady-loves.

It seems probable that the real cause of this conflict of evidence lies in the fact that Gawain's expedition to and residence in the Maidens' Isle (Isle of Women) was an essential part of his story. The lady of his love was really the queen of that other-world, and he was, naturally enough, regarded as the champion of all the dwellers in it. The romances give us no really good reason for the title of '*the Maidens' Knight*,' as ascribed to Gawain; and it does not seem improbable that it may have been part of the original tradition. Gradually, as Christian ideas gained ascendency, this Celtic other-world would come to be looked upon somewhat in the light of a Mohammedan paradise, and the character of Gawain, as dweller in it, suffered proportionately.

Without going so far as Professor Rhys,[2] who looks upon Gawain as a pattern of chastity, and practically equates him

---

[1] Cf. *Hist. Litt.*, xxx. p. 34.

[2] Rhys, *Arthurian Studies*, 'Gwalchmai and Gwalchhaved.' Professor Rhys' explanation of Gawain's rejection of the advances made by the wife of 'the Green Knight' is scarcely in accordance with the character the lady herself assigns to Gawain.

with Galahad, a view which can hardly be sustained by examination of the romances, we may, I think, maintain with truth that the attribution of indiscriminate amours to this knight is not in accordance with original tradition.

The real truth was, I believe, that Gawain's love was not only a denizen of another world, but also, as is frequently the case in such stories, originally *nameless*. It was not till, at a later date, certain attributes of the Goddess of Love had been passed over to the queen of the other-world, that she received a name. Thomas the Rhymer's love is as nameless as the queen who led Bran and Connla to her island court, though Tannhäuser's lady is Venus.

There certainly was a persistent tradition to the effect that Gawain's love was no mere earthly maiden. The traces of such a tradition have, in Chrêtien's poem, been partially, but not entirely, obscured. The circumstances of Gawain's meeting with the lady are in themselves suspicious;[1] she is more or less closely connected with the enchanted castle, and she is certainly nameless. Wolfram's *Orgeluse* is only a misreading of *L'Orgueilleuse de Logres*, the only title by which Chrêtien knows her.

Elsewhere we find it distinctly stated that Gawain's love was a *fairy*. In *Guinglain* or *Le Bel Inconnu*[2] the hero is said to be the son of Gawain and the fairy *Blancemal*. In *Rigomer*[3] Gawain is delivered from prison by the fairy *Lorie*, '*qui moult l'amoit*.' *Florie* is also the name attributed to the mother of Gawain's son in the German *Wigalois*, and in the version P of the *Livre d'Artus*.[4]

---

[1] Cf. remarks on p. 33.
[2] *Hist. Litt.*, p. 176.   [3] *Ibid.*, p. 91.
[4] See note to Dr. Schofield's *Studies on the Libeaus Desconus* p. 236.

In connection with this latter it is interesting to note that the lady is said to be the daughter of the king of *Escavalon*. Now, the lady with whom Gawain had the chessboard adventure was the daughter of the king of Escavalon (Askalon in the *Parzival*), and Wolfram, commenting on the extreme beauty of this lady and her brother, mentions the fact that they came of fairy race.[1] The coincidence is interesting.

Florî is again the name of Gawain's *amie* in *Diu Krône*,[2] though the lady he marries is Amurfina, the niece of Gansguoter, the magician of the enchanted castle. Amurfina is, however, said to be of *Forei*, which may be a reminiscence of *Florî*. We may add to this list of Gawain's fairy mistresses the fay Karmente, who in *Saigremor* detains him in her isle.

But there are two distinct lines of tradition to be noted in the different accounts of Gawain's unearthly love; she is sometimes, as we have seen, a fairy, nothing being said as to her relatives, at others the close connection of a powerful magician. This would appear to have been the case with Chrétien and Wolfram's lady, as it is with Amurfina, whose uncle, Gansguoter, plays the same part as that of the enchanter of the Château Merveil in both French and German poems, viz. that of abductor of King Arthur's mother.

We may remark here that the appearance in this character of the Lord of the Castle finds support in early legend. *E.g.* in Irish tradition, Lug, one of the lords of the Irish other-world, abducts Dechtire, sister of Conchobar, and mother of Cuchulinn, with whom, as we have shown,

---

[1] *Parzival*, Bk. viii. verses 66 *et seq.*
[2] *Diu Krône*, verse 7907.

Gawain has important points of contact. It will be remembered that both in Chrétien and in Wolfram the mother of *Gawain*, as well as of Arthur, is a prisoner in the Magic Castle, and is freed by her son.

That Amurfina is none other than the lady otherwise known as l'Orgueilleuse de Logres, or Orgeluse, seems very probable; and the special interest of Heinrich's presentment lies in the fact that he connects her so closely with the magician. We found in a preceding chapter that Emer, whose wooing by Cuchulinn affords a parallel to the Gawain-Proud-Lady episode, is the daughter of Forgall the Wily, a prince renowned for his magical powers, a feature which suggests an originally closer connection between the magician and the lady in the French and German poems than the authors of those poems were aware of; and which has been, in a measure, preserved in *Diu Krône*.

This relationship however survives, in slightly varying forms, in the English metrical romances. In the fragmentary poem of the *The Marriage of Sir Gawayne*[1] we find the hero, in order to rescue King Arthur from the snares of a powerful enchanter, chivalrously wedding the magician's sister, a lady of unexampled hideousness. On the marriage night she reveals herself as beautiful as she was previously repulsive, and gives her husband the choice whether he will have her beautiful by night, and hideous by day, or *vice versâ*. Gawain, with that courtesy for which he was famous, leaves the decision to the lady; whereupon she tells him she has been laid under a spell to preserve this repulsive form till she finds a knight courteous enough 'to give her her will.' The spell is now broken, and she will be beautiful alike by night and by day.

[1] *Sir Gawayne*, Madden, p. 288.

THE LOVES OF GAWAIN

I am indebted to Mr. Alfred Nutt for having pointed out the existence of a most striking Irish parallel to this story, which, as seeming to indicate the source of the incident itself, and also as strengthening the argument for the Celtic origin of the Gawain legend, we may well insert here. The tale[1] deals with the adventures of the five Lugaids, sons of Dáire Doimtech, one of whom it was prophesied should obtain the kingship of Ireland. 'It had been foretold that the future ruler should bear the name of *Lugaid*, wherefore Dáire, apparently anxious to show no favouritism, gave the name to each of his sons. Pressed for a further indication, the Druid foretold that a golden fawn should come into the assembly, and the son who should take it should win the kingship or sovranty. The fawn appears, and all the sons pursue it; one, Lugaid Laigde (Macniad), caught it, while another brother cut it up. Snow began to fall heavily, and the youths sought for a shelter. They came to a great house, with fire and food in abundance, the mistress of which was a horrible hag. She is ready to give them lodging for the night, provided one of them will share her couch. The youths, not unnaturally, demur at this, but finally Lugaid Laigde (who had caught the fawn) accepts the offer, and the tale runs thus:—*Howbeit the hag went into the couch of white bronze,*

---

[1] This story is translated by Mr. Whitley Stokes in the *Academy*, April 23rd, 1892 (No. 1042), and commented upon by Mr. Nutt in the succeeding number. Mr. Nutt points out that two forms of the story are represented in extant Irish literature, one found in the *Coir Anman* (Fitness of Names), an eleventh-century compilation, purporting to explain the epithets of some 300 famous personages in the older romantic literature; the other found in Annals which cannot be younger than the eleventh century. These two forms differ considerably, and thus testify to the antiquity of the tale.

and Macniad followed her; and it seemed to him that the radiance of her face was the sun rising in the month of May, and her fragrance was likened by him to an odorous herb-garden, and she said to him, "Good is thy journey, for I am the Sovranty, and thou shalt obtain the sovranty of Erin."' The following morning they find themselves horseless, on a level plain, with their hounds tied to their spears.

Now this story is certainly as old as the eleventh century, probably older, and there seems little doubt that in it we have the earliest form of the incident found in the *Marriage of Sir Gawayne*. As Mr. Nutt points out, there is a similar *motif* in the two tales; in the Irish, the lady *is* 'the Sovereignty'; in the English, the question Arthur has to solve is 'What do women most desire?' The answer is 'Sovereignty,' *i.e.* their will. When Gawain practically exemplifies this by giving his bride her own way, the spell is broken.

In the Irish tale the lady herself is the enchanter, and not subject to a spell laid on her by another.

It is an interesting point that both Mr. Whitley Stokes and Mr. Nutt connect this lady with the 'Loathly Messenger' of the Grail, who both in the *Peredur*, and the *Gautier* continuation of the *Perceval* is transformed to a fairer shape. Neither Chrêtien nor Wolfram retain this feature, but the latter, besides his hideous Kondrie, has also a Kondrie *la Belle*; this latter is a resident in the Magic Castle, and is *Gawain's sister*. If she really be, as has been suggested, a survival of the messenger in her transformed shape, the connection with Gawain is curious and interesting. An Irish parallel of certain aspects of this character is Leborcham, the female messenger of King

Conchobar, and one of Cuchulinn's loves; she bore him two sons.

A later version of the English ballad makes the lady the mother of Gyngalyn, known otherwise as *Libeaus Desconus*, and amusingly remarks that though Gawain 'was weddyd oft in his days' yet he never loved any other lady so well. Altogether, this question of Gawain and the Loathly Lady scarcely seems as if it had yet been fully worked out.

Another English romance, *The Carle of Carlile*,[1] in its later form weds Gawain to the 'Carle's' daughter, the hero having previously freed the father from enchantment by striking off his head. It may also be that the amorous advances made to Gawain by the wife of the *Green Knight*, a story with which we shall deal fully later on, owe their origin to a reminiscence of this early feature.

What then, we may ask, is the conclusion to be drawn from this special inquiry? *Firstly*, I think we must admit that Gawain's connection with a lady of supernatural origin is a remarkably well-attested feature of his story. *Secondly*, that between this lady, as represented in the most consecutive accounts of Gawain's adventures, and the queen of the other-world, as represented in Irish tradition, there exists so close a correspondence as to leave little doubt that they were originally one and the same character. *Thirdly*, that in these earlier stories we find, side by side with the lady, a magician, whose connection with her is obscure, but who is certainly looked upon as lord and master of the castle to which she conducts the hero, and which the latter wins. In such stories as the *Carle of Carlile* and the *Green Knight* the character of the magician has been preserved, while the lady has lost her super-

[1] *Sir Gawayne*, Madden, p. 270.

natural qualities. This remark may also hold good for *The Marriage of Sir Gawain*, where the magician is found, but the lady is apparently unable to free herself, unaided, from the spell laid upon her. *Fourthly*, we examined the nature of the castle ruled over by this magician, and we found it to be undoubtedly an 'other-world' dwelling.

Taking all these points into consideration the inference to be deduced from them seems clear—Gawain's love in the earliest instance was regarded as being either the *Daughter of the King of the Other-world*, or as herself the *Queen of that Other-world*. The presence of the magician points to the first of these characters, the parallels with the 'Island of Women' to the second—but, essentially, both characters are one and the same.

It is interesting in this connection to note that Professor Rhys in his *Arthurian Studies* considers Lot, Gawain's father, as having been originally identical with Lug, the Irish Light-god, father of Cuchulinn, and, like Lug, later on a king of the Other-world, or Isles of the Dead. If we are right in the above reading of the problems contained in the Gawain story, the hero was originally a sundeity (therefore probably son of a light-god), and at the same time *son-in-law* to the lord of the other-world.

Another, and not less important, point must also be considered. We saw in the case of the Gawain-Proud-Lady episodes that no parallel to them is found in the *Peredur*, which contains such striking parallels to the *Perceval* portion of Chrêtien and Wolfram's work. Again, in the special features characterising these episodes, which seem to have so far-reaching a bearing on the Gawain story, we have found ourselves compelled to go further back, to seek in *Irish* rather than in *Welsh* tradition for parallels

THE LOVES OF GAWAIN

and explanations—and this search has been fruitful of result. So far as I can speak from personal study, the close connection between Gawain and a magician, or magician's daughter, seems to have completely dropped out of Welsh literature, and yet there seems little doubt that it represents a feature of the primitive story. The French and German romances retain it, so do the English metrical tales. Whence then did they obtain the tradition? The English romances probably drew, at least partially, from French sources; the Germans certainly owed their knowledge of Arthurian legend to France. The question really is, Where did the French poets get their version? Judging from the silence, on so many important points, of Welsh tradition, it seems most probable that, as Professor Zimmer maintains, they obtained their knowledge *direct* from their Breton neighbours, and not from Wales through the medium of England—a view which M. Gaston Paris favours.

It seems probable that this Breton version represented more closely the original form of the story than the tradition preserved in Wales. Otherwise one can hardly account for Chrêtien and Wolfram, not to mention Heinrich von dem Turlin, being in possession of a version so capable of explanation by Irish parallels, which version is at the same time unrepresented in extant Welsh literature. It may be that the Gawain story, thoroughly and carefully examined, will eventually throw important light on the vexed question of the transmission of these fascinating legends.

But, however transmitted, it is, I think, clear that in the solution suggested in these last two chapters we have a key to the conflicting versions of Gawain's amours, as well

54 THE LEGEND OF SIR GAWAIN

as an explanation of that change of character which in the later romances operated so disastrously for his fame.[1]

[1] Mr. Nutt points out that a parallel to this deterioration may be found in the character of Ninian or Nimue, Merlin's love. At first a sympathetic and attractive personality, she gradually, in the expanded Merlin romances, undergoes a change for the worse, developing finally into the repulsive Vivien of the Tennyson Idylls. Kay also declines in the estimation of the romancers, though hardly to the same extent, or on the same lines.

CHAPTER VII

GAWAIN'S SON

Testimony of romances on this point—The Fair Unknown *cycle—General summary of story—Hero's youth—*Libeaus Desconus—Le Bel Inconnu—Carduino—Wigalois—*His connection with Perceval—Views of Dr. Schofield and M Ferd. Lot—His parentage—Superior antiquity of the* Danae *motif—Connection between Gawain and Perceval—Tradition of conflict between father and son—Its bearing on the Gawain legend.*

WE examined in the last chapter the tradition connected with Gawain's love-adventures, and found reason to believe that after all they were perhaps less numerous than the later romances would lead us to suppose. An indirect confirmation of this suggestion may be found in the very scanty references to any offspring of his alleged numerous marriages. Thus, the hero of the group of poems which may be classed together as the *Bel Inconnu* or *Fair Unknown* family, Guinglain, Gyngalyn, or Wigalois, is his son, and Malory mentions two others, Sir Lovel and Sir Florence (Gyngalyn he does not mention), the sons of a lady whom we only know as 'Sir Brandalis' sister.' But M. Ferd. Lot, in a review of Dr. Schofield's *Studies on the Libeaus Desconus,* inclines to the opinion that the son of Brandalis' sister (the earliest accounts only mention *one*) is the same as Guinglain—in which case genuine tradition would ascribe to Gawain only this one son.

56 THE LEGEND OF SIR GAWAIN

The story connected with this hero is found in four leading versions, *Libeaus Desconus* (English), *Guinglain* or *Le Bel Inconnu* (French), *Carduino* (Italian), and *Wigalois* (German). It is therefore a remarkably widespread and popular legend.[1] For our purpose it is only the introductory portion of these romances which is of importance, and it is therefore unnecessary to give a full summary of the hero's adventures, which, briefly speaking, are as follow:—

He arrives at Arthur's court to demand knighthood, and offers his services to a damsel who has come to ask assistance, either from the king or his knights, for her lady. She despises the aid of so young a champion, and flouts him persistently;[2] notwithstanding which the hero boldly overcomes all the dangers of his quest, learns the secret of his parentage, and returns to King Arthur's court to be welcomed with joy by his father, Gawain.

But our special interest lies in the introductory account, which in each poem deals with the hero's history *previous* to his appearance at court. In *Libeaus Desconus* we are told that he is the son of Sir Gawain, 'begotten be a forest side' (which does suggest the adventure with Brandalis' sister); his mother, fearing for his fate if he learnt the use of arms, brought him up alone in the forest that he should see no armed knight. He does not even know his name:

---

[1] Full abstracts of these stories will be found in *Hist. Litt.* xxx., *Le Bel Inconnu* by M. Gaston Paris; and *Studies on the Libeaus Desconus* by Dr. Schofield. I have followed the latter in the summaries given above.

[2] Is it possible that this flouting of the hero by his companion, which is a persistent feature of all the tales of this family (cf. Gareth and Linet and Sir La Côte Maltaile in Malory), may be a reminiscence of the Gawain-Proud-Lady story, having been *transferred from father to son*?

GAWAIN'S SON

He is so fair his mother has only called him *Beau-fis*. One day he finds a knight lying dead in the woods, and clothes himself in his armour. In consequence of this adventure he seeks King Arthur's court.

The *Bel Inconnu* omits the story of the lad's youth, but, like the hero of the English poem, he knows neither his parentage nor his name; his mother has called him *Biel-fil*. The secret of his birth is reserved apparently to heighten the effect of his principal deed of valour, the achievement of the *fier baiser* when he kisses, or rather is kissed by, a horrible serpent, which turns into a fair maiden. Immediately after this a voice reveals to him that he is Gawain's son. The English poem expressly states that the lady could only be disenchanted by a kiss from Gawain, or one of his race.

The *Carduino* is much the fullest in its account of the hero's youth:—Arthur has a favourite noble, who is treacherously slain by some barons of the court (Gawain and his brothers, we find later on). His wife flies with her young son, and takes refuge in a forest, where she brings up the boy in the belief that no other human beings besides themselves exist in the world. He is clothed in skins, and spends his time hunting the wild beasts, slaying them with the aid of two spears he has accidentally found. One day the king and his knights are hunting in the neighbourhood, see the lad, and give chase to him. He escapes, but will live no longer in the forest. His mother accompanies him to a city, where he lays aside his savage dress and is clad in armour. Finally, at the instance of his companions he determines to go to Arthur's court and win honour. Before his departure his mother acquaints him with his father's name and fate.

58 THE LEGEND OF SIR GAWAIN

In the *Wigalois* the commencement is quite different. Gawain has been overcome by an unknown knight, and compelled to follow him to his own land, where he weds the niece of the king. After six months he leaves her to revisit the court, and, the land being enchanted, is unable to find his way back. The boy grows up at his mother's court, where he is trained in all knightly accomplishments, and finally sets out to find his father.

Now on the surface there certainly seems to be a strong resemblance between this story and the well-known *Enfances* of Perceval; and Dr. Schofield arrives at the conclusion that the hero of the romance was originally no other than Perceval himself.

This conclusion M. Lot attacks, but, it seems, on insufficient grounds. He says,[1] 'On retrouve partout des héros dont la jeunesse est obscure, sauvage, ou méprisée. Comme tous ces récits s'influencent reciproquement il nous parait impossible d'espérer atteindre la source la plus reculée.' This is, of course, in a measure true, but we do not see that it operates in the main against Dr. Schofield's theory. It is impossible for any one familiar with the *Perceval* romances not to be struck with the correspondence in detail existing between the two groups: the mother's expressed dread of her son being slain in battle—his absolute ignorance, not merely of his parentage, but of his own name—the very terms of endearment employed by the mother[2]—his being clothed in skins and armed with javelins—the first suit of armour being taken from the body of a dead knight—his giving up his solitary life on his first contact with the outer world and proceeding at

[1] Cf. *Le Moyen Âge*, October 1896.
[2] Cf. *Parzival*, Books ii. verses 1625 *et seq.*, iii. 722-4.

once to Arthur's court. All these features agree so closely that we are surely justified in concluding that the stories forming these two groups represent a common original, even if they be not directly derived the one from the other; *i.e.* if the *Fair Unknown* be not Perceval himself, he and Perceval are both representatives of the same primitive hero, which practically amounts to the same thing.

Of these stories, three, as we have seen, represent the hero as Gawain's son; the fourth, *Carduino*, describes the father as having been slain by three brothers, Calvano, Agueriesse, and Mordarette, *i.e.* Gawain, Agravain, and Mordred; so here Gawain, instead of being the father of the boy, is that father's murderer.

Dr. Schofield considers that the *Carduino* version is later than the others, on the ground, as we understand him, that it represents Gawain in a light quite inconsistent with the early representation of that hero. In this the critic is undoubtedly quite right; it would be impossible to imagine Gawain figuring as a treacherous murderer in any but quite the latest version of his story.

M. Lot, who does not appear to have quite grasped the reasons given by Dr. Schofield for his conclusions, asserts that, on the contrary, the *Carduino* represents the earliest form, giving as one reason for his opinion that 'la vie solitaire du héros est bien mieux motivée.' It is easier, he contends, to understand the flight of a widow, whose husband has been murdered by nobles powerful at court, than to understand the youth's being brought up in ignorance of the fact that he has a famous hero for his father.

But this is, we think, to put the *origin* of the story too late. Both J. G. von Hahn and Mr. Alfred Nutt, in their studies on the *Aryan Expulsion and Return Formula*,[1] have demonstrated that a tale such as this told of Guinglain or of Perceval is of very ancient origin. In the table drawn up by Hahn we find the first feature of such stories to be that the father of the youth is a god, or hero, from afar, while the mother is a princess residing in her own country. Two of the stories classed under this formula are those of Perseus, and Romulus and Remus, both of which introduce the feature classified by Mr. Hartland, in his exhaustive study of the Perseus legend, as the *Danae* motif.[2] The father is a supernatural being, of whose identity the mother herself is not fully aware, and in consequence of her ignorance on this point she and her infant son are expelled from their native land, a feature, as he demonstrates, of extreme antiquity.

There can be no doubt that this represents an older and more archaic type of the story than that in which the father has been killed, either in battle or by treachery; and the fact that the Perceval *enfances* have been recognised as belonging to this family of legends, renders it probable that, at one time or another, this story too presented features conformable to the older type. A proof of this is afforded by the Irish heroic tales. The Ultonian cycle, the chief hero of which, Cuchulinn, is a god's son, is older than the Ossianic, whose hero, Finn's father, is slain. Between the *enfances* of both these heroes and of Perceval a strong resemblance admittedly exists.[3] So far from dismissing the versions

[1] Cf. Nutt, *Aryan Expulsion and Return Formula*; Folklore Record, vol. iv.

[2] Hartland, *Legend of Perseus*, vol. i

[3] Mr. Nutt suggests that the 'Conall' story, in which the father, Art, is both a kingly stranger and is slain, forms an intermediate version.

which represent Gawain as the boy's father as necessarily later than those which represent him as fatherless, it seems not impossible that they may be valuable survivors of a genuine original tradition.

These Studies, dealing, as they do, primarily, with Gawain rather than with Perceval, it will not be necessary to enter into a comparison of the stories connected respectively with this latter and with Guinglain—what has been said above as to the undeniable resemblance between their legends must suffice. What we would ask here is, If Perceval and the *Fair Unknown* resemble each other so strongly as to lead to a suspicion that they are really one and the same, is there any evidence that the first-named was ever regarded as Gawain's son? There does not appear to be any direct evidence on this point, but there are certain points which seem to invite special attention and study.

We may note at first that the tradition as to Perceval's father is extremely vague; he never twice bears the same name, and in many of the romances the hero is generally spoken of as the son of 'la veuve dame.' In fact, the point of Perceval's parentage is undoubtedly obscure.

As we have shown in chapter iii., the early Grail poems closely connect Perceval and Gawain; the romances dealing ostensibly with the former devote quite half their space to recording the deeds of the latter, and, even omitting the fact that Wolfram considers them kinsmen and blood-relations, it seems difficult to explain the close connection of these two heroes—a connection evidently dating from a very early period, and to which no parallel exists in the cycle. In the *Peredur* and the English *Syr Percyvelle* the hero is son to Arthur's sister, and therefore first cousin to

Gawain. Both in Chrétien and Wolfram's poems, and also in the Welsh *Peredur*, it is Gawain who introduces Perceval as a *knight* to King Arthur's court; in the English *Sir Percyvelle* he appears earlier on the scene, and aids the hero to disarm the Red Knight, whom he has slain.

We have already noted [1] that the *Suite de Merlin* [2] contains a statement by the enchanter to the effect that Gawain shall only be overcome by *one* knight. This is undoubtedly Perceval, who in the earliest romances is the only knight whom we find considered in any way superior to Gawain. It is to be noted that there is no growth in Perceval's fame—from the first he is held 'the best knight in the world.'

The *Parzival*, as we have shown, [3] gives an account of just such a conflict between the two knights as is, apparently, indicated by the *Merlin*, a conflict in which Gawain is worsted. This will probably be found to be the earliest instance in which such a fate befalls that originally invincible hero.

It may be well here to recapitulate the details of this conflict: the two knights are unknown to each other, and Gawain is near being slain by his adversary when his pages coming up call on him by name, and Parzival, finding his opponent is his friend and kinsman, throws away his sword with lamentations over the unnatural strife. The maiden Bene, who is acting as go-between in the love-affair between Gawain's sister and King Gramoflanz, rides up at the same moment, and loudly bewails Gawain's evil plight, while at the same time she assists him to the best of her power.[4]

---

[1] Vide *supra*, p. 9.
[2] Sommer, *The Sources of Malory*, p. 105.   [3] Vide *supra*, p. 23.
[4] *Parzival*, Book xiv. verses 274-332 and 390-408.

Now in Malory[1] we find a curious parallel to this combat in a fight between Gawain and his brother Gareth; neither knows the other, and they fight fiercely for over two hours, till the damsel Linet, riding upon a mule, calls on them by name to cease fighting with each other.

A very curious feature in this account is that the adventures of Gareth (or Beaumains), as related by Malory, bear an undeniable resemblance to the adventures of Gawain's son in the *Fair Unknown* stories. The source of this book, Dr. Sommer, in his study on Malory, tells us he has been unable to discover, but he considers that it represents a lost French poem. Without the original before us we cannot tell whether it really formed a link between the *Perceval* and the *Libeaus Desconus* stories or not, but Malory's version certainly seems to touch both.

The special interest as regards these studies is that it renders probable the fact that there *was* a tradition relating to a conflict between Gawain and a near relation, which tradition has been preserved by Wolfram and not by Chrêtien.

We have noted above that, according to the *Merlin*, Gawain was only to be overcome by *one* knight. In the case of a hero so popular, and so generally considered invincible, this knight might be expected to be his own son, as by this means, father and son being practically one, the fame of the original hero would be held to have suffered no diminution. Such a conflict between a father and a son, who do not recognise each other, is of frequent recurrence in old romances, *e.g.* the old German *Hildebrand's lied*, where, however, the father gets the better of the son, while the Celtic hero of such a conflict is none other than

---

[1] *Morte d'Arthur*, Book vii. chap. 3.

64 THE LEGEND OF SIR GAWAIN

Cuchulinn, with whom both Gawain and Perceval have many points of contact.[1]

The question is not one which admits of definite solution; we have not sufficient data for the purpose. The Gawain and Perceval stories certainly came into connection with each other at a very early date, and probably before the latter, at least, was definitely united to the Arthurian cycle; Perceval's connection with King Arthur's court is, in both Chrétien and Wolfram, extremely slight.

We shall probably not be far wrong if we consider these two heroes the earliest to have been brought into contact with the British king; though perhaps we should except Kay, who seems to have belonged to the Arthurian cycle from a very early date, and whose character has, like Gawain's, suffered much in the later romances. We must therefore expect to find the original legend greatly obscured —certainly in the case of Gawain the task of reconstructing the story appears to offer peculiar difficulties, and we cannot hope definitely to solve the problem of the original connection existing between him and Perceval. Their adventures are in themselves so distinct, being entirely unshared the one by the other, that it appears as if we must look outside the letter of their feats for the reason of their union.

The mythical character which Gawain undoubtedly originally bore would not be out of keeping with the father

[1] In the Irish story the father (Cuchulinn) is the victor. The circumstances of the begetting and rearing of his son, Conlaoch, who, when he comes to Conchobar's court, is only known as Aife's son—Aife being his mother,—are not unlike those of the *Bel Inconnu*. Our oldest testimony to the Irish story dates back to the middle of the tenth century, but there can be no reasonable doubt that the incident belongs to the very oldest stratum of Irish story-telling.

of the primitive Aryan hero Perceval is generally held to represent. The story generally told of Gawain's son has many points of contact with the account given of Perceval's youth; further (this may only be a coincidence, but it is a striking one), the hero, who, as we shall see in the next chapter, gradually took in the later Romances the position first assigned to Gawain, has also a son, who for his part supersedes Perceval.

The arguments advanced in this chapter in no sense make claim to be conclusive; all that is claimed for them is that they afford ground for maintaining the hypothesis that these two earliest heroes of Arthurian saga were once looked upon as standing in the relation to each other of father and son, to be not altogether unreasonable, nor entirely devoid of confirmatory evidence.[1]

---

[1] While this chapter was in the press I had the opportunity of reading M. Philipot's important criticism of Dr. Schofield's *Studies on the Libeaus Desconus*, in *Romania* 102, April 1897. M. Philipot agrees with M. Ferd. Lot in regarding Dr. Schofield's identification of *Le Bel Inconnu* with *Perceval* as mistaken, maintaining that the origin of the story is to be sought in the enfances *féeriques* or Lancelot, rather than in the enfances *humaines* or Perceval. Without discussing the question at length, for which a footnote does not afford opportunity, I cannot refrain from saying that I believe M. Philipot to be completely in the wrong in regarding the enfances *féeriques* as anterior to the enfances *humaines*—for these reasons:—

a. The enfances Lancelot have not escaped my notice, but I have hitherto found no Lancelot romance which does not show demonstrable traces of having been affected by the Gawain-Perceval story.

b. In view of the wide diffusion of the central theme of the Perceval story, and the remarkable parallels to be found in other literatures (*e.g.* the Danish Helden Lieder given by Rassmann in vol. i. of his *Helden Saga*, and the accounts of Finn's boyhood in the Ossianic cycle), it is, I believe, a grave error to criticise this story *solely* as a branch of the Arthurian cycle; and it is precisely to the *human* element in the enfances that we find these parallels.

  c. The enfances *humaines* are rougher, more elementary and primitive in character, than the enfances *féeriques*, which are distinctly mediæval and chivalric in type.

  d. I therefore incline to think that the enfances *humaines*, *i.e.* Perceval, represent the older and original version; the enfances *féeriques*, *i.e.* Lancelot, a version due to contamination by the Gawain-Fairy-Mistress traditions; and that the order of evolution was rather as follows:—
(1) Aryan tradition represented by Perceval story (*no* fairy element);
(2) Perceval story affected by Gawain legend = *Le Bel Inconnu* versions;
(3) Fairy element in these versions gradually increasing in importance and issuing finally in the Lancelot version. That the primitive, uncouth, Perceval version, with its curious Celtic and Teutonic parallels, was evolved from the elaborate and finished fairy tale of the Lancelot enfances I cannot believe. The whole question is to my mind a strong and additional argument in favour of what I have further on insisted upon—viz. the necessity for a careful and comparative study of the Lancelot and Gawain Romances.

CHAPTER VIII

LE CHEVALIER DE LA CHARRETTE

Different versions of the story—Chrétien—Hartmann von Aue—Malory—Suggestions as to original hero—Professor Rhys—M. Gaston Paris—Gawain's share in the adventure—The character of Meléagaunt's kingdom—*Li ponz evages*—Pierre Bercheur—Early connection of Gawain and Guinevere—Survival in English metrical romances—Gawain and Lancelot—Perceval and Galahad.

STUDENTS of Arthurian literature are well aware that the poem, the name of which heads this chapter, relates an important episode of the cycle, and one which presents certain specially interesting and perplexing features.

Speaking broadly, it is the story of Guinevere's abduction by a knight named Meléagaunt, and her rescue by Lancelot. Of this story we have several versions. The most famous is that of Chrétien de Troyes—the poem named above. Malory in his nineteenth book relates the story of the *abduction* differently—his source evidently going back to a tradition identical with that preserved by a fragmentary Welsh poem of the fourteenth century; but his account of the *rescue* is the same as Chrétien's.

The *Iwein* of Hartmann von Aue, who in the rest of his poem is following Chrétien's *Chevalier au Lion*, again gives a different version of the abduction, and is silent as to the details of the rescue. The story is also told in the prose *Lancelot*, but this version, as M. Gaston Paris has demonstrated, is directly drawn from Chrêtien's poem.

We have two other accounts of the carrying off of Guinevere; one in the *Lanzelet* of Ulrich von Zatzikhoven, where the abductor is Falerin, and the deliverer Lancelot; the other in *Diu Krône*, where the characters are respectively Gasozein and Gawain.

Inasmuch as Chrêtien's poem is the most widely known we will take this as our standard of comparison.[1] He tells the tale as follows :—A knight appears at Arthur's court, boasting of the ladies whom he holds captive; he will set them all free if Arthur will confide Guinevere to the care of one of his knights, who will undertake a single combat with the new comer (Meléagaunt). If he be defeated all the ladies shall be free; if, on the contrary, the queen's champion is vanquished, Guinevere herself shall become Meléagaunt's prisoner.

Kay, on pretence of being about to quit Arthur's service, demands a boon. This the king promises to grant, and it proves to be that he shall be permitted to accept the challenge. Guinevere goes unwillingly with Kay. Gawain reproaches Arthur, and obtains leave to follow, and free the queen if necessary.

He rides forth in company with other knights; they meet Kay's horse riderless, and covered with blood. Gawain outrides his companions and encounters a knight (Lancelot), who asks him for a steed. Gawain gives him his, and following shortly finds the horse slain, and Lancelot on foot. The latter mounts a cart which they meet, and Gawain follows. The kingdom of Meléagaunt is surrounded

[1] Cf. M. G. Paris's study of the poem in *Romania* x. and xii.

LE CHEVALIER DE LA CHARRETTE 69

by water crossed by two bridges, the one, *pont de l'epée*, a sword-blade, which Lancelot crosses on hands and knees, wounding himself sorely in the crossing; the other, *pont de l'ève*, goes *under* the water. This Gawain selects. Lancelot succeeds in freeing the queen, but falls into a trap set by Meléagaunt, and is himself imprisoned, while Gawain escorts Guinevere back to her husband.

The account given by Chrêtien in the *Chevalier au Lion*, which is very short, agrees with this. The king had put Guinevere in Kay's charge; Gawain has gone to her rescue. It is not stated who frees her, and Lancelot's imprisonment is only incidentally mentioned. In Hartmann's poem, on the contrary, we have an entirely different account of the abduction.[1] A knight appears at Arthur's court and requires the king to grant him a boon—whatever he may ask. Arthur demurs, but finally yields to the knight's taunts and gives the required promise, when the knight demands the queen and carries her off, exactly as the Irish knight Gandîn carries off Queen Isôlt. The knights arm to pursue the ravisher; Kay is the first to overtake him, and is struck from his horse with such violence that his helmet catches in the bough of a tree, and he hangs suspended. He is not taken captive, as in the other versions. One after another all the knights are vanquished, and Guinevere is carried off. *Gawain* is not at court—had he been there it would never have happened; he returns the next day, and rides at once in search of the queen. Later on we are told he has returned to the court,[2] and a few lines further on [3] that in these same days the queen had returned from her captivity. Who freed her is not stated, but we are led to

[1] Hartmann von Aue, *Der Löwenritter*, Book viii. verses 4530-4725.
[2] *Ibid.*, x. verses 5668-9.   [3] *Ibid.*, x. verse 5678.

infer that it was Gawain. Lancelot is not once mentioned throughout the poem.

The differences between the French and German poems are so great that it scarcely seems possible they can be referred to the same source. Nor is it likely that Hartmann would have devoted so much more space to the account of the abduction (two hundred lines as against *ten* in Chrêtien), had he not been dissatisfied with the version of the French poet and desirous of substituting another for it.[1]

Malory's version need not here be taken into account, as it is rather with the latter than the earlier part of the story that we are concerned; and here he agrees in the main with Chrêtien, excepting that Gawain does not appear in the story at all, but the part usually assigned to him is here taken by *Lavaine*. Had the similarity of sound anything to do with the substitution of one name for another?

This story, as the above abstracts show, represents not only a well-known incident of the Arthur saga, but also one of early origin. Like most of the Arthurian stories, it has undergone considerable changes and developments, and it is generally admitted that, as it now stands, it does not represent the original form of the episode; and that, in that original form, it was not Lancelot, but some other hero, who played the part of rescuer.

Who that original rescuer was, critics are not agreed. Professor Rhys in his *Arthurian Studies*[2] equates Lancelot with Peredur (Perceval), and tries to show that the story

---

[1] The German poem is on the whole longer than the French, but by no means so in the proportion indicated by this incident. Chrêtien's poem consists of 6815 verses; Hartmann's of 8165.

[2] Cf. *Arthurian Studies*, chap. vi.

of Guinevere's rescue from Meléagaunt is based upon a mistaken rendering of Peredur's love for the Empress of Constantinople. But it cannot honestly be said that this attempted solution is in any way satisfactory.

M. Gaston Paris, in his study of Chrêtien's Romance,[1] decides that the original hero was Arthur, quoting in support of his opinion a passage in the *Vita Gildæ*, attributed to Caradoc de Lancarvan (about 1150), but, as M. Paris remarks, certainly later. There we are told that Melwas, king of Æstiva Regis (Somerset), carries off Guinevere to Glastonbury. Arthur marches with the armies of Devon and Cornwall to besiege him, but by the intervention of St. Gildas and the Abbot of Glastonbury peace is made, and the queen restored to her husband.

M. Paris admits that the story, as it stands, is a '*déformation monacale d'un récit populaire*,' but maintains, that in representing Arthur as the hero it is in accordance with original tradition. It is with diffidence that one ventures to dissent from the conclusions of such a scholar as M. Paris, but may it not be that it is just in this point of the rescuer that the '*déformation monacale*' is most clearly shown? *i.e.* for purposes of edification the monks substituted the *husband*, who naturally *ought* to have been the deliverer of his wife, for the *lover*, who, in the story as known to them, really freed her—that Arthur is the *last* rather than the *first* of the traditional rescuers?[2]

[1] Cf. *Romania*, xii. p. 511.

[2] We make no use here of the mediæval Welsh fragment quoted by Professor Rhys, *Arthurian Studies*, chap. iii., as it seems impossible to determine its real signification or value. The MS. is apparently of late date, and if it does represent an attempt made by Arthur to carry off his wife from an abductor, the assigning such a *rôle* to him may be only a reminiscence of the 'Gildas' account. This however occurs

It will, we think, be admitted by all Arthurian students that such a feat as the rescue of a lady, Guinevere or any other, from a knight who has carried her off against her will, is not an action attributed, as a rule, to Arthur. It is his knights who perform all these special deeds of chivalry. Arthur is a valiant warrior, a successful general, a slayer of monsters (*e.g.* the giant of Mont S. Michel; and the demon cat in *Merlin*), but not, as a rule, a succourer of distressed damsels. The deeds usually attributed to knights-errant are, on the whole, absent in his story. Further, if Arthur were the original rescuer we should expect to find some trace of this in the later versions, whereas there is no indication that he bestirs himself in the matter; he leaves the pursuit and recovery of his wife entirely in the hands of his knights.

But if the substitution of Arthur for Lancelot does not approve itself as consonant with the indications of the story as we have it, who then was the original hero of the adventure? It seems strange that no one has suggested *Gawain*. Professor Rhys came very near the point when he asked why Lancelot, rather than Gawain, was represented as the queen's deliverer, remarking that Gawain appears in this character in *Diu Krône*; but the Lancelot-Peredur equation with which he was so much in love blinded him to the full force of his own suggestion.

As we have seen above, all the versions, save Malory, represent Gawain, equally with Lancelot, as starting in pursuit of the queen, braving the dangers of the approach

to the mind—the ravisher (if any) in the fragment appears to be Kay. The knight in Hartmann's version carries off Guinevere by a *ruse* identical with that employed by Kay when desirous of accepting Meléagaunt's challenge. Is there any connection between these accounts?

LE CHEVALIER DE LA CHARRETTE

to the castle, and, in the principal version (that of Chrêtien), it is he who brings Guinevere back to the court, and is at first hailed as her rescuer.

In the *Lanzelet* of Ulrich von Zatzikhoven, Guinevere has been carried off by Falerin, and Lanzelet cannot deliver her without the aid of the enchanter Malduc, who refuses to assist him unless Walwein (Gawain) and Erec, with whom he has a feud, are delivered to his power. These heroes voluntarily give themselves up, and Lanzelet, with the aid of the enchanter, frees Guinevere.[1] Here again Gawain plays a not unimportant part in the rescue.

Malory, as we have seen, introduces *Lavaine* into the story, a not insignificant change.

If we couple with this Hartmann von Aue's divergence, apparently of set purpose, from the version given in the poem he was otherwise following; his utter silence as to Lancelot, and apparent inference that Gawain was the rescuer; it must, I think, be admitted that there is *prima facie* sufficient evidence to justify the hypothesis that it was the latter and not Lancelot who was the original hero.

But when we examine the story more closely we shall find this hypothesis much strengthened. Both M. Paris and Professor Rhys are of one mind in regarding the dwelling of Melwas, or Méleagaunt, as an 'other-world' kingdom. Its situation, surrounded by water—the difficulty of access to it—Chrêtien's significant words,

> '*Et si l'a el reaume mise*
> *Dont nus éstranges ne retorne,*
> *Més par force el pais sejorne*
> *en servitude et en essil*'[2]

[1] Cf. *Romania*, x. p. 475.   [2] Cf. *ibid.*, xii. p. 467.

—the identification with Glastonbury,—all point unmistakably to this conclusion.

Now, as we said before (chapter v.), an expedition to such an 'other-world' dwelling is exactly the feat most generally attributed to Gawain. Taking traditional characteristics into question, if there were one of Arthur's knights more likely than another to be represented as the hero of such an adventure as this it would be Gawain.

And surely it is significant that it is he, and not Lancelot, who, nearing the castle, elects to cross by the bridge which, we are told,

> ' A non li ponz evages,
> Por ce que soz eve est li ponz,
> S'i a de l'eve jusqu'al fonz
> Autant desoz comme desus
> Ne deça meins ne de la plus
> Ainz est li ponz tot droit en mi,
> et si n'a que pié et demi
> de lè et autretant d'espès.'[1]

When, in the first version of the story, Gawain rescued the queen, it was doubtless by this bridge, which probably was then the only means of access, that he reached the castle.

In connection with this it must not be forgotten that there exists an independent tradition[2] as to a subaqueous adventure of Gawain. This story, related in the *Reductorium Morale* of Pierre Bercheur, runs as follows:—'What shall I say of the marvels which occur in the histories of Gawayne and Arthur? Of which I will mention only one, namely, of the palace under the water which Gawayne accidentally discovered, where he found a table spread with eatables, and a chair placed ready for him, but was

---

[1] Cf. *Romania*, xii. p. 467.   [2] Vide *supra*, p. 28.

not able to find the door by which he might go out; but being hungry and about to eat, suddenly the head of a dead man appeared in the dish, and a giant, who lay on a bier near the fire, rising up, and striking the roof with his head, and the head calling out, and forbidding the repast, he never dared touch the viands, and after witnessing many wonders, got away he knew not how.'[1]

There is also another reason why Gawain, rather than another, should have gone in search of Guinevere—he was, as we learn from the *Merlin*, specially the 'queen's' knight. This is a boon which he craves for himself and his companions at the first court held after Arthur's marriage. The *Merlin*[2] gives long accounts of the rivalry between the queen's Knights, headed by Gawain, and the Knights of the Round Table—a rivalry which gives rise to more than one fiercely contested tournament.

The English Metrical Romances have preserved this tradition, and when king and queen ride forth, it is Gawain who escorts the queen.[3]

If the carrying off of Guinevere were really a part of the *early* Arthurian legend, it seems scarcely possible to evade the conclusion that it must have been Gawain who rescued her; there was no other knight on whom the duty would have been equally imperative and binding.

[1] This fourteenth-century reference is noteworthy as testifying to the considerable mass of Arthurian romance which has perished, a fact to be borne in mind when the argument, so dear to some scholars, *ex silentio*, is brought forward. The incident itself, so wild and fantastic in character, may be compared to the eleventh-century Irish tale, entitled 'Finn's Visit to the Phantoms,' edited and translated by Dr. Whitley Stokes in vol. vii. of the *Revue Celtique*.

[2] *Roman de Merlin*, chap. xxvi. p. 343.

[3] Cf. *Anturs of Arthur*, verse 1, in Madden's *Sir Gawayne*.

adventure contains a deeper and more interesting problem than the mere identity of Guinevere's rescuer.

If, as here suggested, Gawain, in an early version of his story held the position of the lover of his uncle's wife, we can discover more than one reason which would operate towards the divesting him of such a character. The situation in itself originally belonged to a very elementary stage of society. At first, probably, Tristan was thought no worse of for his *liaison* with Isôlt than was Diarmaid for his abduction of Grainne : the other heroes of Finn's court strongly object to taking any active part against the escaping couple. But at a later period, when the chivalrous ideal of knighthood was fully accepted, and the refinements of *Minne-dienst* as yet undeveloped, such a course of conduct on the part of a trusted kinsman would stamp him as a traitor. The French poets, to whom we owe the development of Gawain's character as a model of knightly courtesy and chivalric virtues, would scarcely have admitted such a flaw in his reputation, even if they knew the story.

We must remember that the method adopted of exculpating Tristan and Isôlt by blackening the character of King Mark, was quite impossible in the case of Arthur, who, from his historical position as leader of the Britons against the invading tribes of heathen Saxons, was naturally regarded as the champion of Christendom and seems in fact to have undergone a steady process of moral and spiritual development, till he culminated in Tennyson's 'blameless king'—a far cry from the original Arthur. It is, I think, clear that if such relations as those suggested above ever existed between Gawain and Guinevere, they must, in the exigencies of the story, have been modified at an early moment. In any case, whether innocent or otherwise, it seems practically certain that a close connection between the queen and her husband's famous nephew did really exist, and taking into consideration the manner in which Lancelot elsewhere supplanted Gawain, I am inclined to think that no 'blundering' on the part of Chrétien or of any other writer need be postulated, but that the story in this special instance only followed the course of development taken by the legend as a whole, and replaced the earlier by the later hero.

It may be asked what proof have we that such a displacement of the one knight in favour of the other ever took place to any appreciable extent? Let any one who doubts the fact read first such romances as Chrétien's *Conte del Graal*, the *Parzival* of Wolfram von Eschenbach, or the *Merlin*, and then turn to Malory's *Morte d'Arthur*, a compilation which, drawn from various sources, gives an excellent general impression of the Arthurian legend in its latest stage. In the first named, they will find Gawain the most valiant of all Arthur's knights, the pattern of courage and chivalry, the pride of the Round Table, and the favourite alike of King and Queen. Lancelot does not come on the scene at all—the *Merlin* just mentions his birth. In all the romances represented by Malory's work (*Tristan*, *Lancelot*, the *Queste*) Gawain is in the background, and it is Lancelot who is the glory of the court, the favourite of the king, the lover of the queen; in fact, he has completely supplanted Gawain.

Such a change did not take place at once, but we can discover indications of the gradual transference of feats from one hero to the other. Thus, in *Diu Krône*[1] we find that Lancelot's strength waxes double at mid-day—a trait which,

[1] *Diu Krône*, verses 2087 *et seq*.

as we have seen, originally belonged to Gawain. Curiously enough, this passage immediately precedes a reference to the story of the '*Charrette*,' here ascribed to Lancelot.[1]

M. Paris[2] notes that in the *Rigomer* he has found a trait attributed to Lancelot which he has not met with elsewhere. He appears in poor attire at an assembly presided over by Arthur, and in order to prove his identity to the knight whom he addresses:

> '*li a la paume tendue,*
> *et cil a le plaie veue*
> *qui saine est et racousturée*
> *Car d'une fort lance acerée*
> *Fu avec le suie* (sic) *ferus.*
> *Par cel est mout reconneus,*
> *n'avait chevalier en Bretagne*
> *ne le conneust par l'ensaigne.*'

[1] M. Paris in his essay on the subject remarks incidentally that the form *Milianz*, given to Guinevere's abductor by Heinrich von dem Turlin, does not represent the French Meléagaunt, and yet that it is improbable that Heinrich knew any other form of the name. Now in the *Parzival*, which Heinrich certainly knew, the name is given as *Meljakanz*; and further, in Book vii of that poem, Meljakanz, and Meljanz von Liz (Melians de Lys), are not only represented as allies in the tournament at Beaurosch, but Meljanz is riding the horse which Meljakanz won from Kay when he smote him out of the saddle with such force that he was found hanging to a bough, verses 588-96. The two names occurring in such close connection, with practically the difference of only one letter between them, a slip of the memory, or of the pen, might easily substitute the one for the other, and this is probably the simple explanation of the puzzling form *Milianz*. It should be stated that Wolfram's reference here is to Hartmann, and *not* to Chrêtien, who has not this incident of Kay's suspension. His subsequent references in the same Book, verses 1471-8, and at the commencement of Book xii. verse 8, are to *Chrêtien's* poem.

[2] *Romania*, x. p. 494.

LE CHEVALIER DE LA CHARRETTE

If such an injury be not elsewhere attributed to Lancelot, we twice over find reference to *Gawain* being wounded in a similar manner.

In *Parzival*[1] we are told how Gawain

> '*mit dem mezzer durch die hant
> stach; des twang in minnen kraft
> unt wert wiplich geselleschaft.*'

And in *Diu Krône*[2] we learn that he pierced his hand through with a knife, in order to rouse himself from a love-trance.

We do not know enough of the sources of *Diu Krône* to say whether the account given by Heinrich was merely invented to explain the *Parzival* allusion, or whether it be a genuine and independent tradition; but it certainly looks as if the original source of the 'Lancelot' incident were to be found in an adventure attributed to Gawain.

In the next chapter we shall discuss an episode which forms the subject of a separate and famous romance of the cycle, and here too we shall find that while one version represents Lancelot as the hero, there is every reason to believe that the story originally attaches to Gawain.

Nor should it be forgotten that the account given by Ulrich von Zatzikhoven of Lanzelet's youth and up-bringing —how he was stolen by a water-fairy, and brought up in her kingdom, *das Meidelant*[3]—presents remarkable points of contact with the Gawain legend. Here too Lanzelet is

---

[1] *Parzival*, Book vi. verses 640-2:
> '*When the knife's sharp blade
> He drove through his hand through love's urging,
> For the sake of a gracious maid.*'

[2] *Diu Krône*, verses 9058-63.

[3] *Romania*, x. p. 473.

represented as Arthur's nephew, his sister's son—a relationship obviously borrowed from Gawain. Elsewhere Lancelot is the son of King Ban of Benoyc, Arthur's valiant ally and friend, but no relation to the British king. The whole question of the relationship of the Lancelot and Gawain stories is particularly interesting, and seems to demand more careful study than it has yet received. *Some* connection between the heroes there certainly must be, but of what nature? Was Lancelot merely an under-study to Gawain? Or is he the hero of an independent cycle of adventures, which, like the Perceval story, early came into contact with the Gawain legend, without remaining, as this latter has done, practically unaffected thereby? There seems reason to believe that Lancelot was a comparatively late addition to the *Arthurian* story; the earliest romances, as we have seen, know nothing of him.

The question becomes doubly interesting when we take into consideration the relation between Perceval and Galahad. That the *former*, and not Galahad, was the original Grail winner is practically certain, and his suppression in favour of Galahad presents a remarkable parallel to the suppression of Gawain by Lancelot. Galahad was Lancelot's son. If, as suggested in the previous chapter, Perceval was once considered as son to Gawain, we have the interesting problem of one pair of heroes, originally father and son, being displaced by another pair, bearing the same relationship to each other, and to the characters of the original story: Gawain = Lancelot, Perceval = Galahad.

There are certain circumstances connected with Galahad which seem to lend colour to such a supposition, however far-fetched it may at first appear. His mother, too, is a princess residing at her father's court; his father, a hero from afar, a mere passing guest. His birth takes place under remarkable circumstances; he is brought up apart from his father, and the latter, though he confers knighthood upon his son, is ignorant of his identity, till he arrives at court, and declares his relationship to King Pelles. There seems here to be an echo of the tradition originally connected with Gawain's son, and with the Aryan hero represented by Perceval.

But this digression has led us somewhat astray from the original subject of our study—the freeing of Guinevere. The considerations advanced above go, we think, far towards proving that the original hero of the adventure was neither Lancelot nor Arthur, but Gawain. In all the versions he appears as playing a part only secondary to Lancelot; in one, Hartmann's, we are led to infer that he, and he alone, achieved the adventure; the only version which does not name him at all introduces a comparatively obscure knight of a similar name. The story, in its original significance,[1] is exactly in accordance with the feat most generally attributed to him, and the very details of his journey to the castle conform to the primitive '*données*' of his story. If we reject Lancelot as the primitive hero, as scholars are generally agreed to do, we must, I think, admit that the body of evidence in favour of Gawain is far stronger than can be advanced in the case of any other knight.

[1] It may be noted that the ladies, who are reported to be also held prisoners by Meléagaunt, are not mentioned again; they seem to drop out of the story as we have it. But the fact that they are mentioned forms an interesting parallel to the Château Merveil story, where, besides the queens, a number of ladies are also captive.

We might even be justified in holding that the very fact that it is *Lancelot* who is here represented as achieving an adventure which apparently reaches back to a very early stage of the Arthurian legend, is in itself an argument in favour of *Gawain*—he being the hero whose place in the cycle Lancelot gradually usurped.

Whether the story is old enough to be considered as having formed part of the *original* Gawain legend is another question, and one which cannot be positively answered. It seems probable that it did not do so, but that its analogy to a feat which *did* belong to that original legend caused it to be attributed to the hero of the older story.

CHAPTER IX

SIR GAWAIN AND THE GREEN KNIGHT

Summary of the English poem—*Li Conte del Graal*—*Diu Krône*—*La Mule sans Frein*—The prose *Perceval*—The *Fled Bricrend*—Antiquity of the story—Comparison of the various forms—Examination of the *Carados* version—Identification of the Knight-Magician—Original significance of the story—Probable order of the different versions—The magic girdle—The story probably a genuine survival of original Gawain legend.

AMONG the Metrical Romances, which, as we have already said, formed, previous to Malory, the English contribution to Arthurian literature, the most important is that known as *Syr Gawayne and the Grene Knyghte*; important not only from the point of view of literary merit, which is considerable (M. Gaston Paris considers it '*le joyau de la litterature Anglaise au Moyen Âge*'), but also from its subject-matter—the adventure which it relates being found in varying forms in other romances, and, there is reason to believe, going back to an early stage of Celtic saga.

As the story, while it preserves with singular fidelity its archaic character, is yet given at greater length, and with more elaboration, in the English poem than in the other versions, we will first consider the adventure as there related, and then compare the other accounts with it, thus endeavouring to discover what were the original features of the story, and who was its earliest hero.

86   THE LEGEND OF SIR GAWAIN

The poem, as given by Sir F. Madden in his *Sir Gawayne*, is printed from a MS., believed to be unique, in the Cottonian collection. From internal evidence it appears to have been *written* in the reign of Richard II., *i.e.* towards the end of the fourteenth century, though it may have been composed somewhat earlier; and the authorship has been ascribed to the Scottish poet, Huchown, whose *Morte d'Arthur*, preserved in the Lincoln Library, was used, among other romances, by Malory in his compilation.[1]

The story is as follows:—On a New Year's Day, while Arthur is keeping his Christmas feast at Camelot, a gigantic knight, clad in green, mounted on a green horse, and carrying in one hand a holly bough, and in the other a 'Danish' axe, enters the hall and challenges one of Arthur's knights to stand him 'one stroke for another.' If any accept the challenge he may strike the first blow, but he must take oath to seek the Green Knight at a twelve-months' end and receive the return stroke. Seeing the gigantic size and fierce appearance of the stranger the knights hesitate, much to Arthur's indignation. Finally Gawain accepts the challenge, and, taking the axe, smites the Green Knight's head from the body. To the dismay of all present the trunk rises up, takes up the head, and, repeating the challenge to Gawain to meet him on the next New Year's morning at the Green Chapel, rides from the hall.

Faithful to his compact, Gawain, as the year draws to an

---

[1] Cf. Madden, *Sir Gawayne*, p. 299 *et seq.* Mr. Gollancz, on the other hand, assigns the poem to the author of *Pearl* and other middle English alliterative poems of a didactic character, and regards the whole group as belonging to the West-Midland district, *i.e.* to the borderland between the English-Welsh-speaking lands. See his edition of *Pearl*, London, 1892.

GAWAIN AND THE GREEN KNIGHT 87

end, sets forth amid the lamentations of the court to abide his doom, which all look upon as inevitable. He journeys north, and on Christmas Eve comes to a castle, where the lord receives him kindly, tells him he is within easy reach of his goal, and bids him remain over the feast as his guest. Gawain accepts. The three last days of the year the host rides forth on a hunting expedition, leaving Gawain to the care of his wife, and making a bargain that on his return they shall mutually exchange whatever they have won during the day. Gawain is sorely tempted by the wiles of his hostess, who, during her lord's absence, would fain take advantage of Gawain's well-known courtesy and fame as a lover. But he turns a deaf ear to her blandishments, and only a kiss passes between them, which he, in fulfilment of his compact, passes on to the husband on his return. The next day the result is similar: Gawain receives and gives two kisses. The third day, besides three kisses, the lady gives him a green lace, which, if bound round the body, has the property of preserving from harm. In view of the morrow's ordeal, from which Gawain does not expect to escape with his life, he cannot make up his mind to part with this talisman, but gives his host the kisses, and says nothing about the lace. The following morning at daybreak he rides forth, and comes to the Green Chapel, apparently a natural hollow, or cave, in a wild and desolate part of the country. The Green Knight appears, armed with his axe, and bids Gawain kneel to receive the blow. As the axe descends, Gawain instinctively flinches, and is rebuked for his cowardice by the knight, who tells him he cannot be Gawain. The second time he remains steady, but the axe does not touch him. The third time the knight strikes him, inflicting a slight cut on the neck.

88 THE LEGEND OF SIR GAWAIN

Gawain promptly springs to his feet, drawing his sword, and announces that he has now stood 'one stroke for another,' and that the compact is at an end; whereon the Green Knight reveals himself as his erewhile host. He was cognisant of his wife's dealings with Gawain; the three strokes equalled the three trials of his guest's fidelity, and, had not Gawain proved partially faithless to his compact by concealing the gift of the lace, he would have escaped unharmed. The name of the Green Knight is Bernlak de Hautdesert, and he had undertaken this test of Gawain's valour at the instance, and by help of the skill, of Morgan le Fay, who desired to vex Guinevere by shaming the Knights of the Round Table.

Gawain returns to court, tells the whole story, concealing nothing, and all the knights vow henceforward to wear a green lace in his honour.

This is a summary of the wild and fantastic story, the origin of which Sir F. Madden believed he had discovered in the first continuation (by Gautier de Doulens) of Chrêtien's *Conte del Graal*. But this theory, though at first favourably received, cannot, we think, be maintained.

In the French poem the story is connected with a certain Carados, Arthur's nephew, and the son, unknown to himself, of a powerful enchanter. This latter makes his appearance as does the Green Knight (only he is not dressed in green, and the colour of his steed is 'fauve'), while Arthur is holding high court, at Pentecost—not at Christmas. He is armed with a sword instead of an *axe* (which latter seems to be the original weapon), and proceeds at once to explain to Arthur what he means by 'one blow for another'—viz. that he will allow one of Arthur's knights to cut off his head on condition that he may be allowed at a year's interval to do the same for the knight. This, M. Gaston Paris observes, at once marks a corrupted form of the story, revealing as it does the superhuman nature of the challenger.

But we are not sure that this does not really correspond to the original form, *only*, and this is an important difference, in the primitive version the hero knows from the first that it is a magician with whom he is dealing, and there is no masquerading in the form of a knight. This will become clear as we proceed in our investigation. To proceed with the story:—All refuse, with the exception of the new-made knight, Carados, who, in spite of the remonstrances of king and queen, seizes the sword and strikes off the knight's head. The latter takes it up, replaces it on his shoulders (not riding off with it in his hands, as in the English poem), and, bidding Carados look for his return in a year's time, departs. At the expiration of the year the knight returns and finds Carados ready to submit to the test, but at the prayer of the queen and her ladies he forbears the blow (thus omitting the real test of the valour of the hero), and reveals the true relationship, that of father and son, between himself and Carados.[1]

It seems difficult to understand how any one could have regarded this version, ill-motived as it is, and utterly lacking in the archaic details of the English poem, as the *source* of that work. It should probably rather be considered as the latest in *form*, if not in *date*, of all the versions.

Two other accounts, which seem, so far as can be judged from the comparison of an abstract with an original to be practically the same, again connect the story with Gawain.

[1] *Conte del Graal*, vol. iii.

lot shall cut off his head, taking an oath that he will return in a year's time and submit to the same ordeal. Lancelot complies, and the knight falls dead. At the expiry of the year the hero returns, and is met by the brother of the first knight. Lancelot kneels down, commends his soul to God, and prepares to receive the blow; but as the axe descends he flinches, and is rebuked by the knight—'So did not my brother.' Before he can strike again two damsels interpose, and at their prayer Lancelot's life is spared. Twenty knights have already been slain without their slayer having dared to keep his part of the compact by returning. Lancelot's courage, and fidelity to his word, have broken the spell; the 'Gaste Cité' is re-peopled.

It will be seen here that there is no trace of a magician, and it is evidently a late form of the story.

We have already referred (chapter vi.) to the story of Gawain disenchanting the Carle of Carlile by striking off his head; and in Malory's Seventh Book, previously quoted, we find Gareth, Gawain's brother, arriving at the castle of his lady, Dame Liones. During the night he is attacked by a knight in armour, and strikes off his head. The knight is healed by an ointment applied by the damsel Linet, and returning the following night, fights again with Gareth, is again beheaded and restored to life by the same means. The story seems to lack point, and both it and the *Carle of Carlile* incident are probably reminiscences of the 'Green Knight' legend.

But to all appearance the oldest version now accessible is that of the *Fled Bricrend* (Bricriu's Feast), an Irish tale preserved in MSS. written towards the end of the eleventh or beginning of the twelfth century, but representing a tradition considerably older, and showing no trace of Christianity.[1] The story there given is as follows:—

The three heroes, Cuchulinn, Loégairé, and Conall, dispute as to which of them is entitled to the chief place and 'portion of the hero' at the feast. The king, Conchobar, declines to decide the question himself, and after appealing to several judges, they are finally referred to the giant Uath Mac Denomain, who dwells near a lake. They seek the giant, and submit the questions to him. He promises a decision if they, on their part, will observe a certain preliminary condition—which they undertake to do.

This proves to be of the nature of a bargain—'Whoever of you says Uath will cut off my head to-day, and allow me to cut off his to-morrow, to him shall belong "the portion of the hero."'

Loégairé and Conall either refuse to submit to the test, or having cut off the giant's head fly without waiting for the return blow, there appear to be two versions—Cuchulinn, on the contrary, declares himself willing to submit to the test. Uath, giving his axe to Cuchulinn, lays his head on a stone, the hero smites it from the body, and the giant, clasping it to his breast, springs into the lake. The next morning he reappears, whole as before. Cuchulinn presents his neck to the axe. The giant makes three feints at striking him, and pronounces that he has fulfilled the conditions, and is alone entitled to 'the portion of the hero.'

The versions of Irish sagas preserved in the eleventh- and twelfth-century MSS. seem not infrequently to contain 'doublets' of the same incident, and thus at the conclusion

[1] This account is taken from the notes to M. G. Paris's study on 'Sir Gawain and the Green Knight,' *Hist. Litt.*, xxx. p. 77. Cf. for a detailed summary of the tale, Zimmer, *Kelt Studien*, v.

of the *Fled Bricrend* the incident occurs again, in a fragmentary form in the oldest MS. (the Book of the Dun Cow), but complete in a later MS. from which it has been translated by Professor Kuno Meyer.[1] This version differs from the one given above in a manner important for our inquiry. The stranger, a gigantic figure, carrying axe and block, arrives at the court of Conchobar during the absence of the three heroes, Cuchulinn, Conall, and Loégairé. He excludes the king, and his councillor Fergus, from his challenge, but directs it to all the other heroes. The terms agree with the earlier version. The first who accepts is Munremar, who smites off the stranger's head; he takes it up, and departs with it in his hand. The following night he returns, but Munremar does not appear to fulfil his part of the bargain. The chief heroes are, however, present, and declare their readiness to accept the challenge. Loégairé and Conall follow Munremar's example in evading the fulfilment of their pledge; Cuchulinn, as before, comes triumphantly through the ordeal. The giant only strikes him *once*, with the blunt edge of his axe, and proclaims him the chief hero of Ulster. He likewise reveals his own identity; he is Curoi Mac Dairé, the famous Munster warrior and magician, to whom the settlement of the supremacy of the Ulster champions had been remitted by Ailill and Medbh, whom Conchobar had first chosen as judges of the matter.

It will be seen here that the *conditions* of the test resemble more closely those of *Diu Krône* and *La Mule sans Frein*; but the *three* blows of the oldest Irish MS. are only found in the English version.

The story is then an exceedingly old one, and the first

---

[1] Cf. *Révue Celtique*, vol. xiv. p. 455.

recorded hero with whom it is connected is the Ultonian hero Cuchulinn. We have already noted the many striking resemblances between this hero and Gawain; it seems therefore, *prima facie*, likely that if the story were connected with one of the knights of the Arthurian cycle, it would be with that one who is admittedly of Celtic origin, and moreover already connected with Cuchulinn; and when we examine the stories as they have descended to us, we find that the three versions ascribing the adventure to Gawain undeniably present more archaic features than either of the remaining two—*two* out of these three giving the challenge in the same terms as in the Irish stories; in *one*, the *Mule sans Frein*, the opponent of the hero is a giant, while in the *Green Knight* he is of gigantic size, thus again recalling the primitive version.

Further, it is significant that in the two remaining versions the hero is in one instance a young knight of whom little or nothing is known, but who is here said to be *Arthur's nephew*; in the other, the very knight who, as we saw in the last chapter, gradually superseded Gawain, *i.e.* Lancelot.

But so much has been claimed for the *Carados* version, which, as we said above, has been held to be the source of the English poem, that it cannot fairly be put on one side without a careful examination of the reasons for so rejecting it. As a point in favour of its priority it has been held that the close relationship between magician and hero, there existing, represents a feature of real antiquity which has dropped out, even of the Irish story. The father of Cuchulinn, the primitive hero of the adventure, was not merely a god, but also one of the *Tuatha de Danann*, a god turned magician.

96 THE LEGEND OF SIR GAWAIN

This is true so far as it goes, but the point for us is, Was the giant who tested the valour of the Ultonian hero represented in *any* version as being that hero's father? If he were, no trace of it has come down to us, and it seems creating unnecessary confusion to postulate such a lost version, when, as we hope to show, the evidence all points to a much simpler solution.

If it be true that Cuchulinn was the son of a magician, it is also quite as true that he married a magician's daughter. The real question seems to be, Which of the two characters does this weird enchanter of the Green Knight story represent—the hero's father or his father-in-law, the lord of the Château Merveil?

On this point the *Diu Krône* version, which, as we have seen, agrees in the terms of the challenge with the *Fled Bricrend*, and possesses some specially archaic features, is very explicit—the magician is Lord of the Magic Castle, abductor of King Arthur's mother, and uncle to the lady whom Gawain eventually marries.

Nor are indications of this lacking even in the *Carados* version. The story there told of the *liaison* between the mother of the hero and the enchanter closely resembles the account of the loves of Klingsor, lord of the Château Merveil, and Iblis, wife of the king of Sicily, as related by Wolfram.[1] The English poem, as we noted in a preceding chapter, seems also to have retained a hint of this, in the relations between Gawain and the wife of the knight-magician, who exerts all her fascinations to induce the hero to make love to her. The *Carle of Carlile* story, which relates how Gawain struck off the *Carle's* head, thus freeing him from

[1] Cf. *Parzival*, Book xiii. verses 895-910. See also notes to English translation of *Parzival*, vol. ii. p. 213.

enchantment, and wedded his daughter, belongs to the same group, and adds its testimony to strengthen the suggested identification.[1]

But if the magician of the story *was* originally the lord of the Château Merveil, then we have, I think, a clear indication of how the story first came to be connected with *Gawain*: *it was one of the tests he had to undergo in order to prove himself a worthy mate for the enchanter's daughter.*

Connected with Cuchulinn, the point of the story was clear and definite; it was no mere vague, chance adventure; there was something to be won by submitting to the ordeal. Why transfer *this*, among all Cuchulinn's innumerable feats, to Gawain, unless he, too, was to be tested for a definite purpose? This original *motif* of the story has dropped out, but the idea that the trial was designed as a special test of Gawain's valour still survives.

And, if this was really the original meaning of the story, I do not think it is difficult to see how the magician came in the French poem, and in that alone, to be represented as the hero's *father*. The version of the story known to the poet had lost the lady, for whose sake the feat was undertaken, altogether. There is no trace of the magician's

---

[1] Having nothing but an abstract of *La Mule sans Frein* before me, I cannot tell whether there the giant who tests Gawain's valour is in any way connected with the lady on whose behalf he rides on his quest. If any scholar familiar with the original could supply information on this important point I should be very grateful.

It is noteworthy, in connection with the suggestion thrown out in the two preceding paragraphs, that a love-adventure between Cuchulinn and Blathnaid, wife of Curoi, was one of the most famous love-stories of ancient Ireland. The Ulster hero is at first overcome and imprisoned by the Munster champion, but, thanks to Blaithnaid's help, he ultimately succeeds in killing the husband and carrying off the wife.

daughter here surviving. At the same time it is possible that the idea of a near relationship between magician and hero still lingered, and the author, either of the *Carados* version, or of its source, accounted for this relationship in a manner accordant with the story he already knew of the enchanter's *liaison* with a queen. If we reject this, which seems an easy and natural solution, and prefer to consider the French story as a genuine survival of the connection between the Ultonian hero and his supernatural father, *then* we must postulate, (*a*) the existence of a hypothetical original, differing in at least one important point from the *Fled Bricrend* story, (*b*) that this original descended by a different line than that of the Gawain versions, where the Magician=Lord of the Magic Castle, and the hero's father-in-law.

Now we are tolerably certain that this was not the case, for not only is there a similar story told of the enchanter in the French poem to that told of the Lord of the Castle, but the hero is *Arthur's nephew*, i.e. the tale *has* been affected by the Gawain versions.

In estimating the relative value of the versions, as representatives of the original form, it is interesting to note that they fall apparently into two classes, in one of which the magician seeks the hero, and the scene passes at Arthur's court, in the other the hero goes to find the magician (or meets him accidentally), and the adventure falls out at the castle of the latter.

Now this variation of form *may* correspond to the two versions of the *Fled Bricrend*, in one of which Cuchulinn seeks the giant in his home, in the other the giant comes to Conchobar's court, or it *may* be due to the growing popularity of the Arthurian legend, which encouraged the placing of such adventures in the brilliant frame provided by the famous court. If the former were the case we should expect to find very little difference in detail and character between the two groups. As a matter of fact, those which have kept the visit *to* the magician offer, as a rule, much more archaic features, though we must except from this rule the prose *Perceval*. The oldest form of the story may therefore be said to be represented by the Book of the Dun Cow version of the *Fled Bricrend*, *Diu Krône* and *La Mule sans Frein*; in these three cases the hero visits the magician, and the blows are given on succeeding days.

The *Green Knight* poem, which represents the magician seeking Gawain at Arthur's court, and Gawain visiting the magician for the return blow, is an ingenious combination of the two forms,—the only version we possess which does attempt to combine them. The introduction of a year's interval between the two strokes is probably due to this variation, which necessitated a double journey, on the part of the magician and on that of the hero. The author of the *Green Knight*, or his source (probably his source), was either the first to make the magician visit Arthur's court (if due to the influence of the Arthurian legend), or already knew *two* forms of the story. The original author of the *Carados* version, on the other hand, only knew *one*, and that not the oldest form. So he never suggests the visit of the hero to the magician, and keeps the year's interval between the blows, for which, in his case, there was no need, as they were to be given on the same spot. The challenger might just as well have returned the next day, as he does in the *Fled Bricrend* continuation, which seems to show that the visit to the court was not due to a knowledge of that early variant.

100 THE LEGEND OF SIR GAWAIN

Further, the knight in the French poem is armed with a *sword*, not with an *axe*, which was undoubtedly the original weapon; he replaces his head on his shoulders, instead of going off with it in his hand, a touch which adds much to the weird horror of the original story; finally, and this is the most decisive proof of all, the return blows are entirely omitted, so the hero is spared the real and crowning test of his valour, a test which, unless we greatly mistake, was the *raison d'être* of the whole story. On all these grounds there seems little doubt that the story, as told by Chrêtien's continuator, represents a very late, and eminently unsatisfactory, version of this popular adventure.

The *Perceval* or *Lancelot* version, on the other hand, though manifestly late, is much better motived. There is a real test of the hero's courage in his returning after a year's interval to face what is, practically, certain death; nor is he spared the ordeal of the return blows. But the fact that the challenger is no magician, but is really slain, shows conclusively that the author had only a late and confused form of the story before him.

So far as we can tell, taking the Irish story as our basis, the *Diu Krône* and *Mule sans Frein* versions are the oldest, the *Lancelot* the youngest of the series. *The Green Knight* and the *Carados* versions come in between them, and the English poem is certainly the older of these two.

This, of course, would practically settle the point of the identity of the original hero, did not the fact that the feat belongs to the Cuchulinn-Gawain parallels place it beyond doubt. It is Gawain and 'not Lancelot nor another' to whom it should rightfully be ascribed.

There is one interesting feature in the story, which hitherto does not appear to have attracted much attention, viz. the *lace* which the wife of the Green Knight bestows upon Gawain, and which has the power of conferring invulnerability on its wearer. In *Diu Krône*, too, we find Gawain in possession of a magic girdle, wrought by a fairy, which also has the power of preserving the wearer from harm. Gawain apparently wins it to give to Guinevere; but the story is confused, and it is evident from numerous allusions in the poem that he himself retains, if not the *girdle* itself, the *stone* in which its magic power resides, and which is eventually won from him by a trick.

We find the girdle again in the *Wigalois*, when a knight appears with it at the Court, offering it as a gift to Guinevere; bidding her, if she will not accept it, to send a knight to fight with him. Guinevere at first takes the girdle, but the following day, by Gawain's advice, returns it. One after another the stranger overthrows all Arthur's champions. Finally, Gawain himself is overcome, and forced to ride with the new comer to his own land. On the way the knight gives the girdle to *Gawain*. This hero weds the niece of the king of the land (as we saw in chapter vii.), and it is because he has parted with this girdle, which is enchanted, to his wife, that he cannot find his way back to her.[1] The story is not very clear, but the point of importance for us is that here again we find this hero possessed of a magic girdle.

Now *Cuchulinn* also had such a girdle, and scholars have seen in the powers conferred by it a connection with the invulnerability generally ascribed to the northern hero Siegfried. It seems therefore not unlikely that this feature, preserved only in the English poem, may also be referred

[1] Cf. Dr. Schofield's abstract of the poem *Libeaus Desconus*. *Studies*, p. 235.

to an early Celtic source. In any case it is undoubtedly interesting, and seems to demand closer examination.

On the whole, the adventure which we have discussed in this chapter stands on a different footing to that which we studied in the preceding. There, the conclusion seemed to be that, though there was a strong body of evidence in favour of Gawain as the original hero, yet that that evidence was not of a character to lead us to conclude that the story need necessarily have formed part of the *original* Gawain legend.

Here it is otherwise. There is practically no doubt that, as connected with Arthurian legend, it was Gawain, and Gawain alone, who was the hero of the adventure. The Celtic parallels are strong evidence for an early date, and in more than one version we find traces of a connection with the adventure which demonstrably formed part of the primitive Gawain story, *i.e.* the *Château Merveil* episode. Taking all these points into consideration, there seems strong grounds for concluding that in the stories classed under the heading of this chapter we have a genuine survival of a feat which formed part of the very earliest adventures attributed to the hero,—if we mistake not, one of the special deeds of valour by which he won the favour and the hand of his 'other-world' bride.

CHAPTER X

THE LEGEND IN MALORY

Importance of Malory's version as drawn from all the principal branches of Arthurian literature—Testimony of each section to early Perceval-Gawain story—Passages in illustration—Their bearing on the relations between Chrétien and Wolfram—Concluding summary of results deduced from these Studies.

In concluding these Studies it may be interesting to note the various passages in Malory's compilation, which, drawn as they are from widely differing sources, seem to indicate a very general knowledge of the legend as related by Chrétien and Wolfram.

Some of these passages have already been noted, but it will be useful to give them more fully, and also in a collected form. Thus, we have noted (chapter v.) that the adventure of a knight reaching an island ruled over by a queen, vanquishing the knight who defends the island, and then finding himself compelled to take his place till he, in his turn, be vanquished, ascribed to Gawain in the Romance of *Méraugis de Portlesguez*, is in Malory[1] ascribed to Balan. A special detail in this adventure is that the conflict is watched by the ladies of the castle: 'thenne Balyn looked up to the castle and saw the towres stand full of ladyes.' This detail seems to connect the conflict with that fought

[1] *Morte d'Arthur*, Book ii. chap. 18.

104 THE LEGEND OF SIR GAWAIN

by Gawain before the Château Merveil;[1] the fact that the ladies in the castle are spectators of the jousts ridden without is strongly emphasised in the *Parzival*.

Again, Malory[2] gives an account of how Gawayne, Uwayne, and Marhaus, riding together, come to the *Country of straunge auentures*. 'In this country sayd syr Marhaus cam neuer knyghte syn it was crystened / but he fonde straunge auentures / and soo they rode / and cam in to a depe valey ful of stones / and ther by they sawe a fayr streme of water / aboue ther by was the hede of the streme a fayr fontayne / and thre damoysels syttynge therby /. And thenne they rode to them / and eyther salewed other / and the eldest had a garland of gold aboute her hede / and she was thre score wynter of age / or more and her here was whyte vnder the garland / The second damoysel was of thyrtty wynter of age with a serkelet of gold aboute her hede / The thyrd damoysel was but xv yere of age / and a garland of flowres aboute her hede/.'

Professor Rhys[3] compares these ladies with the well-maidens mentioned in the introduction to the *Conte del Graal*—but surely they are no other than the three queens of the Château Merveil? Age and appearance correspond

---

[1] Cf. *Parzival*, Books x. verses 979-84, xii. 430-2, 470-3, xiii. 165-171. Dr. Oskar Sommer has already suggested that when the stories of Balan and of Gawain are closely investigated, the two heroes will be found to be connected with each other. The fact that the crowning incident of the former story is the fight between Balan and his brother Balin, in which the two, unknowing, mortally wound each other, may therefore lend aid to the hypothesis above advanced, *i.e.* that such a conflict with a near relative was part of the early Gawain story.

[2] *Morte d'Arthur*, Book iv. chap. 19.

[3] Cf. *Arthurian Studies*, chap. xii.

THE LEGEND IN MALORY 105

exactly.[1] Chrêtien especially mentions the white hair of the eldest queen. Their position by a fountain, at the head of a rough and rugged ravine, recalls the deep ravine with river running through it, which Gawain has to cross to gather the garland for his Proud Lady—while the 'Country of straunge aventures' = *Terre Márveile*, as the land is called in the *Parzival*, where we also read, *gar âventiure ist al diz lant*.[2] This Fourth Book of Malory is devoted specially to the adventures of Gawain, though other knights are introduced.

Both this and the Second Book are taken from the *Merlin* Romance in its extended form, viz., the 'Ordinary' *Merlin* and the *Suite de Merlin*.

The adventure of Sir Bors in the Grail Castle[3]— 'Ande thenne Syre Bors layd hym doune to reste / and thenne he herd and felt moche noyse in that chamber /— shot of arowes and of quarels soo thick that he merveylled / and many felle upon hym and hurt hym in the bare places / and thenne—cam in an hydous lyon,' etc., is of course Gawain's adventures in the '*Lit Merveil.*' Malory's source here is the prose *Lancelot*.

So in Book xiii. chap. 7, where Gawain is the first of all the knights to vow himself to the quest of the Holy Grail —a feature not at all in accordance with his general character in this romance—we recall the fact (of which this is doubtless a reminiscence) that in the earliest versions it was Gawain and Perceval *alone* who were represented as undertaking the quest.

But the most interesting proof of the survival of the

---

[1] *Conte del Graal*, Potvin, vol. iii., verses 9273, 9475.
[2] Cf. *Parzival*, Books xi. 126, x. 1360.
[3] *Morte d'Arthur*, Book xi. chap. 5.

early version, and seemingly a decisive one for the establishing of the mutual independence of the French and German poems, is found in Book xiv. chapter 1 (taken from the *Queste*), where Perceval comes to a hermitage inhabited by a female recluse. He kneels down before the window, and the recluse opens it, and talks to him through it—finally revealing herself as Perceval's aunt.

Now, an exact parallel to this incident is found in the *Parzival* (Book ix. verses 65 *et seq.*), where the hero arrives at a hermitage in a forest, and finds it inhabited by a maiden; he speaks to her through the window, she recognises him, and finally reveals herself as his cousin *Sigune*.

Chrêtien, on the contrary, knows nothing of any *female* recluse related to Perceval. The hermit is his uncle, as he is elsewhere.

The *Queste* also gives Perceval a *sister* of a holy and 'devoted' life. The question is, How did this tradition arise? There is nothing in Chrêtien's poem to account for it; there is no reason to believe that the writer of the *Queste* knew the *Parzival*; and yet it is clearly evident that Walter Map (if it really was he who wrote the *Queste*) and Wolfram von Eschenbach were on this point both in possession of a substantially identical tradition. The conclusion seems certain, viz., that there was a *French* version of the *Perceval*, and (as the incidents referred to previously would indicate) of the *Gawain* story, agreeing with Chrêtien's version in the main, but differing in detail.

That the author of the *Queste* knew the old *Perceval* story seems quite clear; the aunt was queen of the ' *Waste Lands*'—a name which recalls ' *la gaste forest Soltaine*' (*Soltane*) of Chrêtien and Wolfram. Perceval's mother

THE LEGEND IN MALORY

dies of sorrow at his departure, as in both these versions.

The fact that when Perceval in the *Queste* reaches the castle of Carbonec (the Grail Castle) he sees through a grating an aged man upon a bed, reminds us that in the *Parzival* he sees, through a doorway, the maimed king's father:

> *An eine spanbette er sach*
> *in einer kemenâten*
> *ê si nâh in zuo getâten*
> *den allen schoensten alten Man*
> *des er kunde ie gewan,*
> *ich magez wol sprechen âne guft*
> *er was noch grawer dan der tuft.*[1]

Whereas in Chrêtien he does not see the Fisher King's old father at all.

And this impression is borne out by other references to the original story,[2] *e.g.* in a passage, found both in the prose *Lancelot* and the *Tristan*, we are told how on Perceval's arrival at court he is seated among the least renowned knights, when one of the queen's maids, '*who has never said a word,*' suddenly begins to cry out, 'Sergent de notre Seigneur ihesucrist vierge et net, viens te seoir au siege de la table ronde empres le siege perilleux'—and taking Perceval by the hand, leads him to the seat.

Dr. Sommer[3] connects this incident with Chrêtien, saying

---

[1] Cf. *Parzival*, Book v., verses 504 *et seq.*
> '—— *and lo! thro' the open door,*
> *Within another chamber, on a folding couch he saw*
> *The fairest of old men ancient whom ever his eyes had seen,*
> *Grey was he as mists of morning—nor o'er rash is the tale, I ween.*'

[2] *Morte d'Arthur*, Book x. chap. 23.

[3] Cf. *Sources of Malory*, p. 199.

that it occurs in his poem, but this is a mistake. Chrétien knows of the damsel who has never *laughed*, but nothing of a *dumb* person, knight or maiden. Wolfram, on the other hand, beside the laughing damsel, Kunnewaare, has a knight, Antanor, who has sworn never to speak till the damsel laughs, and is therefore called '*the Silent.*' Doubtless there was a tradition of a dumb person speaking known to the writers of the prose romance, but they did *not* get it from Chrétien.[1] The Welsh *Peredur* has two dwarfs who have not spoken for a year. The feature of Kay having mocked at Perceval on his first appearance at court is also preserved by Malory, being referred to in Book xi. chapter 12, drawn, Dr. Sommer states, at secondhand from the prose *Lancelot*.

In Malory's Third Book, the source of which is the *Suite de Merlin*, we are told how King Pellinore, Perceval's father, riding on a quest, meets a lady with a wounded knight in her arms. She beseeches his aid, which he, eager to achieve his quest, delays to give. The knight dies, and the lady slays herself for grief. She is Pellinore's own daughter, and, therefore, Perceval's sister. This can hardly be other than a reminiscence of Perceval's cousin, nameless in Chrétien, Sigune in Wolfram, whom he meets under similar circumstances.

The special interest of such passages as are here given from Malory lies in the fact that this work is avowedly a compilation drawn from all the principal branches of the Arthurian cycle—the *Merlin*, the *Lancelot*, the *Tristan*, and the *Queste*. Now, as we have seen, the references to the Gawain and Perceval legend, as related by Chrétien and Wolfram, are not confined to any *one* of these branches,

[1] The fool and his companion, chastised by Kay, are not dumb.

but are found in books drawn from *all*. The legitimate conclusion is that this form of the story was early and widely known; and, although overlaid by later accretions, had left so deep an impress on the traditional conception of these two heroes as to influence, more or less strongly, every version that has descended to us.

If not the *original* legends, they must certainly represent a very early and widely known version of the stories.

Further, it appears that in the case of some of the most striking parallels the agreement is with the *German* rather than with the *French* poem. We cannot believe that the writers of the different prose romances knew the *Parzival*, which, popular as it undoubtedly was in its own land, exercised no influence outside Germany. We are therefore led to the conclusion that side by side with Chrétien's version of the story of these early Arthurian heroes there existed another, deriving from a source identical with, or analogous to, that of the French poet, but apparently fuller in detail.

That Chrétien's poem was not the *original* fount of the Perceval-Gawain story we know. Are we necessarily bound to believe that no eyes but his ever saw the book lent to him by the Count of Flanders?—that he possessed an entire monopoly of the original source?

In Arthurian criticism hitherto there has been far too much of what may be called the 'Chrétien *plus* Imagination' theory, *i.e.* that theory which attributes any episode resembling an episode in Chrétien to that poet as source— explaining all variations of detail, however important, to the imagination of the borrower. The story of the *Green Knight*, which we discussed in the last chapter, is a case in point. That the influence exercised by Chrétien's works in the extension and development of the Arthurian legend was unequalled by those of any other writer may be freely admitted, but the sources used by Chrêtien also went for something in that development; and we make a grave mistake when we pursue our researches as far back as the French poet, and no further.

Thus, instead of setting the *Parzival* outside the range of our inquiries, as being a mere replica of the more widely known *Perceval*, we shall do better to examine it side by side with the French poem as bearing independent testimony to a parallel stream of French tradition. Our ground of examination will become thereby both wider and stronger.

What was said in the opening chapter may with propriety be repeated here on the closing page. It is only by examining singly and in detail the stories of each of the knights who formed the court of the hero, King Arthur, that we can hope to arrive at a satisfactory conclusion as to the growth and development of this important cycle.

These *Studies* have attempted to at least clear the ground for such an examination of the Gawain legend, and though necessarily partial, for so wide a field cannot all be explored at a first attempt, it may, I think, be claimed that we have arrived at certain definite and helpful results.

In the first place, the parallel between Cuchulinn and Gawain has proved to be no mere accidental resemblance, confined to perhaps an isolated adventure, but a substantial thread, running more or less persistently through the whole series of studies, and meeting us, as in the case of the magic girdle, sometimes in unexpected places. And even when the parallel with the Ultonian hero did not appear, other Celtic evidence, as in the case of the *Island of*

Women and *The Marriage of Syr Gawayne*, was amply forthcoming. That the ultimate *source* of the Gawain story was Celtic there can scarcely be further doubt.

We have thus been enabled to demonstrate that one special adventure, with strongly marked 'other-world' features, formed a very early part of his story, and was on the whole more widely known in connection with him than was any other adventure.

Into the framework offered by this story it seems probable that other incidents, now apparently detached, originally fitted. The *Green Knight* story is a case in point; not improbably the *Marriage* incident may have once done so.

This framework, the achievement of a series of feats in order to win the hand of a supernatural bride, was eminently elastic; it would be quite possible for any early singer of Gawain's deeds to lengthen the roll of the hero's exploits by the introduction of feats taken from varying sources. May it not be that in the theory here suggested we have, not only a well-attested basis from which to continue our investigation, but also an explanation of the crowded and conflicting nature of the tradition which has gathered round the name of King Arthur's famous nephew?

INDEX

ABBOT OF GLASTONBURY, 71.
Æstiva Regis (Somerset), 71.
Agravain, 10, 59.
Agueriesse. See Agravain.
Ailfe, 64 n.
Ailill, 94.
Amurfina, wife of Gawain, 47; ?same as l'Orgueilleuse de Logres, 48, 90.
Antanor, the Silent, 108.
Anturs of Arthur, 75 n.
Art, 60 n.
Arthur, legend of, 1-6; French, German, and English treatment, 2 seq.; Malory, 2, Tennyson, 2, Historical, 3-4; Comes Britanniæ, 4; Mythical, 4; Arthurian Knights—Gawain, 5-6; Gift of Excalibur to Gawain, 16, not as a rule rescuer of ladies, but slayer of monsters, 72; Development of hero, 78.
Artusius. See Arthur.
Askalon, 20, 47.
Avalon, Abode of the Dead, 34.

BALAN Compare Gawain, 39, 103.
Balin (also Balyn), 103, 104 n.
Ban, King, father of Lancelot, 82.
Beaumains, Gareth, 63.
Bene, 63.
Benoyc, Kingdom of Ban, 82.
Bernlak de Hautdesert, name of Green Knight, 88.
Blancemal, 46.
Blathnaid, Wife of Curoi, 97 n.
Bleeding Lance, 20.
Bors, Sir, 108.
Bran, Voyage of, 37, 38, 41, 46.

Brandelidelein, 23.
Brandalis' sister, Mother of Gawain's sons, 55.
Branstock, (Sword of.) Compare with Excalibur, 16.
Bricriu's Feast. See Fled Bricrend.

CALADBOLG. See Excalibur.
Caledvwlch. See Excalibur.
Caliburnus. See Excalibur.
Calvano. See Gawain.
Camelot, 86.
Caradoc de Lancarvan, 71.
Carados, 88, 89, 95, 96, 99.
Carbonec. See Grail Castle.
Carduino, 56, 57, 59.
Carle of Carlile, 28, 51; compare with Green Knight, 92, 96.
Castle, Abode of the Dead, 34, 42; magic, see Château Mervil.
Caxton, 3.
Château Merveil, 19, 21, 22, 24; chapter v., 40, 41, 47, 50, 83, 96, 97, 98, 102, 104.
Chaucer, 39.
Chevalier au Lion, 9 n, 67, 69.
Chevalier de la Charrette, 28, chapter viii.
Chrêtien de Troyes, 2; Earliest record of Gawain, 8, 9 n., 11, 16, chapter iii., 22, 24, 26, 32, 33, 36, 46, 47, 53, 63, 67, 68, 73, 79, 88, 105, 106, 107, 108, 109.
Cimetière Perilleux, 27, 28.
Clarions, First owner of Gringalet, 14.
Comes Brittanniæ. See Arthur.
Conall, 60, 93.
Conchobar, uncle of Cuchulinn, 29, 30, 47, 51, 64 n, 93, 97, 98.

H

Cond, 37.
Conlaoch, 64 *n.*
Connla, 37, 41, 46.
Cuchulinn, compared with Gawain, 17; Wooing of Emer, 28, 30, 47, 51, 52. Compared with Finn, 60, 64 and *n.*, 77, 93, 94, 95, 96, 97, 98, 100, 101, 110.
Curoi, 97 *n.*
Curoi Mac Dairé, 94.

Dáire Domtech, father of the Lugaids, 49.
Dechtire, mother of Cuchulinn, 30, 47.
Demoiselle du Gautdestroit. *See* Orgeluse.
Diarmaid, flight with Grainne, 77, 78.
Diu Krône, 20 *n.*, 27, 28, 36, 37, 42, 45, 47, 48, 68, 72, 79, 81, 90, 91, 94, 96, 99, 100, 101.
Dover Castle, 3.
Dwarf (hideous), 21; (dumb), 108.

Emer, wooing by Cuchulinn, 28, 29, 48.
Erec, 15, 45, 73.
Escalibur. *See* Excalibur.
Escavalon. *See* Askalon.
Excalibur, solar hero, 15, compare with Sword of Branstock, 16, Zimmer, on, 16, won from King Rion, 17; Gift of Lady of Lake, 17; three distinct swords, 17.

Falerin, 68, 73.
Fair Unknown, chap. VII., 55, 59, 61, 63.
Fergus, councillor to Conchobar, 94.
Feud Quest, 42.
Fier-baiser, 57.
Finn. Compare with Perceval and Gyngalyn, 60, 75 *n.*, 77, 78.
Fled Bricrend, 92 *seq*, 96, 98, 99.
Florence (Sir), son of Gawain, 55.
Flori, mother of Gawain's son, 46, 47.
Forei, 47.

Forgall the Wily, father of Emer, 29, 48.
Freyr, his steed, 15.

Gaheris, 10.
Galahad, 5, 7, 16, 45 *n.*, 46, 82.
Galvanus. *See* Gawain.
Gandîn, 69.
Gansguoter, uncle of Amurfina, 47, 90, 91.
Gareth, 9, 10; (or Beaumains), 63, 92.
Gasozein, 68.
Gautier de Doulens, 12, 50, 88.
Gauvain. *See* Gawain.
Gauvain et l' Echiquier, 28.
Gawain, previous to Malory, more fully represented in English literature than Arthur, 2; Skull at Dover Castle, 3, 5-6; Different names, 7; close connection with Arthur, 8; earliest mention and early ideal, later degeneration, 8 *seq.*; Malory inconsistent, 9; compared with Tristan, 10; Origin, 11; Characteristics and story, 12 *seq.*; Variation of strength during day, 12, solar divinity, 13; steed, 14, 15; sword, 15, 16, 17; Parallels with Cuchulinn, 17 (*see also* Cuchulinn); Perceval or Conte del Graal and Parzival, earliest stories, 18 *seq.*; Bleeding lance or Grail, 20; Le Chateau Merveil and Lit Merveil, 21 and 32 *seq.*; Orgeluse, 22; Perilous Ford, 22; Vengeance de Raguidel and Cimetière Perilleux, 27; Water adventure, 32, 74; Magic Island, 34; in Fairyland, 39; compare with Balan, 39, his ghost, 39; not a Grail but a Bleeding-Lance Hero, 42; no special love story, 44, Maidens' Knight, 45; Son, 55, 59; Fight with Gareth, 63; mythical, 65; Rescuer of Guinevere, 72 *seq.*; Queen's knight, 75; compare with Lancelot, 76, 79, 82; Adventure with Green Knight, chap. IX.; quest of Holy Grail, 105.

INDEX

Gawayne (Marriage of Syr), 28, 48, 50, 52.
—— (Syr) and Grene Knyghte, chap. IX.
Geoffrey of Monmouth, 1.
Geraint. *See* Erec.
Gilbert, connection with Gringalet, 15.
Gingalet. *See* Gringalet.
Girdle, also lace, 87, 101, 110.
Glastonbury, 3, 71, 74.
Gottfried von Strassbourg, 2
Grail-bearer, 42; -Castle, 19, 20, 42, 105, 107, Conte del or Perceval, chap. iii.; -Holy, 5, 10, 20; -legend of, 9; -quest, 24, 79, 106, 107, 108; -winner, 82.
Grainne, flight with Diarmaid, 77, 78.
Gramoflanz. *See* Guiromelans
Grani, compared with Gringalet, 15.
Green Knight, 45 n., 51; Adventure with Gawain, chapter ix, English Poem, 85-88; named Bernlak de Hautedesert, 88; French version, 88-89; German, Diu Krône, 90; French, compare with Carle of Carlile, 92; Fled Bricrend, oldest version, 92; Lace or magic girdle, 101, 111.
Gringalet, Steed of Gawain 14, 15; Various spellings, 15; Merlin, on, 14; won from Clarions, 14; meaning lost, 15; only once in Welsh literature, 15; Professor Zimmer, on, 15, compare with Grani, 15, 21; theft of, 27.
Guillaume d' Orange (Roman de), 39.
Guinevere, 10, 67 *seq*, 73; carrying off and rescue, 71, 72, 75, 77, 78.
Guingalet. *See* Gringalet.
Guingambrésil or Kingrimursel, 19, 20.
Guinglain, 27, or Le Bel Inconnu, 46, 56.
Guiromelans, 22, 23, 37, 62.
Gwalchmai. *See* Gawain.
Gyngalyn, son of Gawain, 51; story of, 56 *seq*.; called Beau-fis or Biel-fil, 57.

HARTMANN VON AUE, 2, 9 n, 67, 69, 70, 73, 80 n., 83.
Heinrich von dem Türlin, 20 n, 48, 53, 80. *See also* Diu Krône.
Hermodur, deliverance motif, 41.
Hildebrand's lied, 63.
Huchown, 86.

IBLIS, 96.
Island, of the dead, 34, 52; magic, 38; of women, 36, 40, 45, 52, 111.
Isölt (Queen), 45, 69, 76.
Iwein, contest with Gawain, 9; in Fairyland, 39, 67.

KARMENTE (Fairy), 39, 47.
Kay, 5, 23, 64, 68, 69, 72 n., 80 n., 108 and n.
Keincaled. *See* Gringalet.
Kingrimursel (or Guingambrésil), 19.
Klingsor, 34, 96.
Kondrie, 50.
Krône Diu. *See* Diu Krône.
Kunnewaare, the laughing Damsel, 108.

LACE. *See* Girdle.
Lady of Lake, connection with Excalibur, 16, 17.
Lancelot, 5, 10, 38, 44, 65, 66 n., 67, 68, 69, 70; rescuer of Guinevere, 72, 73; Queen's lover, 76, 77, 79; in Rigomer, 80; supplanter of Gawain, 81 and *seq*.; son of King Ban, 82; Green Knight, adventure, 91, 100, 105, 107, 108.
Lanzelet. *See* Lancelot.
Lavaine, 70, 73.
Le Bel Inconnu. *See* Guinglain.
Leborcham, female messenger of Conchobar, 50.
Le Gringalet. *See* Gringalet.
Libeaus Desconus, 51, 55, 56, 63, 65 n., 66.
Linet, 63, 92.
Liones (Dame), 92.

Lit Merveil, 21, 105.
Livre d'Artus, 46.
Loathly Lady, 51.
Loathly Messenger, 19, 50.
Loégairé, 93, 94.
l'Orgueilleuse de Logres. See Orgeluse.
Lorie (Fairy), 46.
Lot, identical with Lug, 52.
Lovel (Sir), son of Gawain, 55.
Lug, father of Cuchulinn, 30, 47, 52.
Lugaid Laigde (Macniad), 49.
Lugaids, sons of Dáire Doimtech, 49.

MACNAID. See Lugaid Laigde, 49.
Maidens' Knight, 45.
Malduc, 73.
Malory, 2, 3; inconsistent with regard to Gawain, 9, 10, 13, 39, 40, 55, 63, 67, 70, 72, 79, 85, 86; great importance, chap x.
Map (Walter), 106.
Marhaus, 104.
Mark (King), 78.
Medbh, 94.
Meidelant (das), 37, 81.
Méleagaunt (also Melwas), abduction of Guinevere, 41, 67, 68, 69, 71, 73, 80 n., 83 n.
Melians de Lys. See Milianz.
Meljakanz. See Milianz.
Meljanz von Lys. See Milianz.
Melwas. See Méleagaunt.
Méraugis de Port les guez, 28, 39, 103.
Meriaduc, 28.
Merlin, 8, 9, 13, 14, 16, contest between Perceval and Gawain, 62, 63; 72, 75, 76, 79, 105, 108.
Milianz, abductor of Guinevere, 80 n.
Mordarette. See Mordred.
Mordred, 10, 59, 77.
Morgan le Fay, 88.
Morris (William), 11.
Morte d'Arthur. See Malory and Huchown.
Mule sans Frein (la) Green Knight story, 90, 91, 94, 95, 97 and n., 99, 100.

Munremar, 94.

NIBELUNGENLIED, 34.
Ninian (or Nimue), 54 n.; compare Vivien.

ODIN, connection with Gringalet, 15.
Oisin, 37, 41.
Orgeluse, Gawain's chosen Lady, 22, 23, 27 n., 28, 46.
l'Orgueilleuse de Logres,
l'Orgueilleuse pucelle, 48.
Ossianic cycle, 60, 65 n., 77.

PARZIVAL, 14, 18 seq., 23, 28, 34, 35, 40, 62, 76 n., 79, 80 n., 81, 96 n., 104 n., 105, 106, 107, 109, 110.
Pearl, 86 n.
Pelles (King), 83.
Pellinore (King), Perceval's father, 108.
Perceval, 5, 13, chap iii 24, 42; compare with Gyngalyn, 58, 60, 61, 62, 63, 64, 65 and n.; Perceval Galahad, 82, 83; Green Knight story, 91; Quest of Holy Grail, 105, 106, 107, 108, 109, 110.
Perceval li Gallois, 28.
Perceyvelle (Sir), 61.
Peredur, 30, 50, 52, 61, 108.
Perilous Ford, 22.
—— Glen, 29
Pierre Bercheur, 28, 74.
Plain of Ill-luck, 29.
Pont de l'epée, 69.
—— de l'éve, 69.
Proud Lady, 22, 28.

REDUCTORIUM Morale, 28, 74.
Renouart, 39.
Rigomer, references to Gawain, 27, 46; Lancelot, 80.
Rion (King), Excalibur won from, 16, 17.
Roland in Fairyland, 39.
Roman de Guillaume, 39.
Ross, 8.

INDEX

SAIGREMOR, 27, 39, 47.
Scathach, 29.
St. Gildas, 71.
Siegfried, 15, 34 *n.*; comparison with Gawain, 38, 77, 101.
Sigune, 106, 108.
Sigurd, deliverance motif, 41.
Sovereignty (the), 50.
Swipdag, deliverance motif, 41.
Swords, 15-17.

TANNHÄUSER, 41, 46.
Tennyson, 2, 11, 54 *n.*, 78.
Thidrek-saga, 34.
Thomas the Rhymer, 41, 46.
Tristan, 5, 10, 11, 38, 44, 76, 78, 79, 107, 108.
Tuatha de Danann, 95.

UATH MAC DENOMAIN, 93.
Ulrich von Zatzikhoven, 68, 73, 81.
Ultonian Cycle. *See* Cuchulinn.
Uwayne, 104.

VENGEANCE de Raguidel, 27, 28.
Venus, 46.
Vita Gildæ, 71.
Vivien, 54 *n.*
Voyage of Bran. *See* Bran.

WALWEIN. *See* Gawain.
Wigalois, 9, 46, 56, 58, 101.
William of Malmesbury, 8.
Wolfram von Eschenbach, 2; chap. iii., 24, 32, 36, 37, 40, 41, 46, 47, 50, 52, 53, 61, 63, 64, 90, 96, 101.
Wooing of Emer, 28, 29, 48.

INDEX OF AUTHORITIES

Bartsch (K.), 14.
Gollancz (I.), 86 *n.*
Hahn (J G. von), 59.
Hartland (E. Sydney), 60.
Lot (Ferd.), 55, 58, 59, 65 *n.*
Madden (Sir F.), 5, 6, 10, 16, 28 *n.*, 39, 48 *n*, 51 *n*, 75 *n.*, 86, 91.
Meyer (Prof. Kuno), 29, 37 *n.*, 94.
Nutt (Alfred), 4, 5, 28, 37 *n.*, 49, 50, 54 *n.*, 59, 60 *n.*, 77.
O'Grady (Standish Hayes), 77 *n.*
Paris (M. Gaston), 5, 7, 8, 9, 11, 14, 28 *n.*, 45, 53, 56 *n.*, 68, 71, 73, 76, 80 and *n.*, 85, 89, 93 *n.*

Philipot (E.), 65 *n.*
Potvin (Ch), 12 *n.*, 105.
Rhys (Prof), 4, 45, 52, 70, and *n.*, 72, 73, 104 *n.*
Rajna (Signor), 8.
Schofield (Dr.), 9 *n.*, 46 *n.*, 55, 56 *n.*, 58, 59, 65 *n.*, 91 *n*, 101 *n.*
Sommer (Dr Oskar), 4, 40, 62, 63, 63 *n.*, 104 *n.*, 107, 108.
Stokes (Whitley), 49 *n.*, 75 *n.*, 50.
Strachey (Sir Ed.), 10.
Zimmer (Prof.), 5, 8, 14, 15, 16, 30, 53, 93 *n.*

Printed by T. and A. CONSTABLE, Printers to Her Majesty
at the Edinburgh University Press

A LIST OF WORKS
ON THE
ARTHURIAN ROMANCE AND ON CELTIC LEGEND
Published by DAVID NUTT in the Strand.

Malory's Morte D'Arthur. Edited by Dr. H. Oskar Sommer.

The 'Morte D'Arthur' is not only a monument, unsurpassed in many ways, of English prose, it must always remain the best means of access to the Arthurian romance, Britain's greatest contribution to the world of imaginative fiction. Dr. Sommer's edition is the only one which provides an accurate text and a full apparatus for the critical and literary study of Malory's compilation.

Sommer's 'Morte D'Arthur is complete in 3 vols. 4to (Vol. I. Text; Vol. II. Glossary, Index of Names and Places, etc.; Vol. III. Study on the Sources); costing together £2, 10s. net, in stiff wrappers, or £3 in Roxburghe binding.

To place this great monument of English literature within reach of all students, Vol. I. (the Text), a magnificent 4to of 800 pages, may be had in plain wrapper at 7s. 6d. cash (8s. 3d. post free).

Studies on the Legend of the Holy Grail. With especial reference to the hypothesis of its Celtic origin. By Alfred Nutt. 10s. 6d. net.

[Nearly out of print.

The Legends of the Wagner Drama. ('The Niebelungen,' 'Parsifal,' 'Lohengrin,' 'Tristan,' 'Tannhäuser.') By Jessie L. Weston. 6s.

The Parzival of Wolfram von Eschenbach. Translated for the first time into English Verse, by JESSIE L. WESTON. 2 vols., 15s. net.

Wolfram's 'Parzival,' upon which Wagner founded his music-drama of 'Parsifal,' is the most interesting and individual work of mediæval literature prior to the 'Divina Commedia.' In addition to her rendering Miss Weston discusses the poet's sources, and artistic and ethical treatment of his theme, so as to bring out the full importance and significance of this great work.

The Vision of Mac Conglinne. Irish Text, English Translation (revision of Hennessy's), Notes and Literary Introduction. By Professor KUNO MEYER. Crown 8vo. 1892. liv–212 pp., cloth, 10s. 6d.

One of the curious and interesting remains of mediæval Irish storytelling. A most vigorous and spirited Rabelaisian tale, of equal value to the student of literature or Irish legend.

The Voyage of Bran, Son of Febal, to the Land of the Living. An Old Irish Saga, together with numerous other Irish Texts of the 8th—10th centuries, now first edited, with Translation, Notes, and Glossary. By KUNO MEYER.

With Essays upon the Irish Vision of the Happy Otherworld and the Celtic Doctrine of Rebirth. By ALFRED NUTT.

Section I: THE HAPPY OTHERWORLD. Crown 8vo, xvii–331 pp Printed on laid paper. Cloth, uncut, 10s. 6d. net.

Section II: THE CELTIC DOCTRINE OF RE-BIRTH. Crown 8vo, xii–352 pp. Cloth, 10s. 6d. net.

Lightning Source UK Ltd.
Milton Keynes UK
UKHW021130140721
387153UK00005B/935